ABOUT THE AUTHOR

JOHN FITZHUGH MILLAR received his A.B. from Harvard in 1966 and his M.A. from the College of William & Mary in 1981. He has taught at three colleges and has been a museum director in Newport, Rhode Island. He has spent years studying various aspects of life in the sixteenth, seventeenth and eighteenth centuries, such as architecture, decorative arts, classical and folk music, dance, ships and military history, and he has lectured extensively on these subjects. He first learned Country Dancing from George Fogg of Boston and studied the more historical aspects under Leland and Gail Ticknor of Williamsburg. He dances with the Williamsburg Heritage Dancers of Williamsburg, Virginia, both for recreation and for hire.

His major published works include:

THE ARCHITECTS OF THE AMERICAN COLONIES (*now out of print*), 1968

RHODE ISLAND: FORGOTTEN LEADER OF THE REVOLUTIONARY ERA (*Providence Journal Books*), 1975

COLONIAL & REVOLUTIONARY WAR SEA SONGS & CHANTEYS (*Folkways Records FH5275*), 1975

SHIPS OF THE AMERICAN REVOLUTION TO COLOR (*Bellerophon Books*), 1976

AMERICAN SHIPS OF THE COLONIAL & REVOLUTIONARY PERIODS (*now out of print*), 1979

A COMPLETE LIFE OF CHRIST (*Thirteen Colonies Press*), 1985

EARLY AMERICAN SHIPS (*Thirteen Colonies Press*), 1985

ELIZABETHAN COUNTRY DANCES

By *JOHN FITZHUGH MILLAR*

Thirteen Colonies Press

Williamsburg, Virginia

1985

Thirteen
Colonies Press
710 South Henry Street
Williamsburg, Virginia 23185

Library of Congress Catalogue Number 85-51583

ISBN   0-934943-00-1 paperback
        0-934943-03-6 hardcover

This book is set primarily in eleven-point Sabon, which is a modern, readable recutting of the sixteenth-century Garamond type. The
paper is a smooth white approved by the Library of Congress for its
long life.

Books of *Historical* interest, covering primarily from the Renaissance to 1800.

INTRODUCTION

If a group of Americans were stationed on a remote island, one could be sure that they would take with them some baseball equipment or perhaps a football, while a similar group of Europeans would probably take some soccer balls.

An English group in that situation from the middle of the sixteenth century until the early nineteenth century would have taken Country Dancing with them. Before the popularity of most of today's ball-centered sports, dancing was a favorite and customary recreation for the English and indeed for most Westerners.

In Elizabethan England, three distinct forms of dancing flourished side by side. Traditional ritual dances, whose origins are buried probably at least as far back as the Druid era, were generally confined to participation by one sex at a time—usually men—and may have been intended to entertain or propitiate the gods enough that crops would thrive and harvests be plentiful. Such ritual dances include the celebrated Abbots Bromley Horn Dance from Staffordshire and the Padstow Mayers' Hobby-Horse Dance from Cornwall. Also under this heading are the ritual-like Morris Dances. The actual origins of Morris Dancing have been the subject of considerable debate and speculation; one school of thought held that Morris comes from the Spanish word Morisco and hence that Morris Dancing is related to some African or Arab ritual, but John Forrest, in his *Morris and Matachin* (Sheffield, 1984), has laid to rest many of the myths.

In 1578, Sir Walter Ralegh's ship *Falcon* was separated from a fleet of ten ships; he intended to explore the coast of North Carolina and the Chesapeake region before proceeding to Newfoundland, but the ship never arrived in America because he turned back when the crew ran out of wine. In a deposition in a lawsuit relating to the voyage, Fernandes the pilot stated that among the goods aboard the ship (which may have been used to purchase more wine in the Canary Islands) were "certain morys belles" (certain Morris bells)—part of a Morris Dancer's attire; thus, Morris Dancing had to wait until later before it could be unleashed on an unsuspecting North America.

The second form of dancing current in Elizabethan England was what is loosely called Court Dancing. Much Court Dancing was very intricate, elaborate and energetic, and it was confined almost exclusively to the nobility. Court Dances, which included the Coranto or Courante, the Almain, the Pavan, the "lascivious" Lavolta and, most impressive of all, the Galliard, were, like the much later Minuet, danced by one couple at a time, either alone or in procession, who did not interact with others. The Court Dances were imported from continental Europe, and the importance of learning them had been impressed on an earlier generation when Henry VIII had met with the French king François I at the Field of the Cloth of Gold near Calais. The directions for quite a few of these dances survive in a handful of English manuscripts, mostly between 1570 and 1670, and in a remarkable French book of 1588, *Orchesographie* by Thoinot Arbeau (anagrammatic pen-name for Jehan Tabourot), of which a modern, paperback edition has been published by Dover.

Queen Elizabeth took a keen interest in dancing, and was not alone among European rulers in choosing her advisors from among dancers; Sir Christopher Hatton is said to have received his post as a result of his dancing abilities. Elizabeth continued her own dancing to the end of her long life; the Spanish ambassador disapprovingly reported that "the head of the Church of England and Ireland" danced three or four strenuous galliards in her old age at the Twelfth Night Revels of 1599. However, in 1661, the young Louis XIV of France, who loved dancing, realised that it was in his best interest to keep his skillful dancers separate from his skillful advisors on government policies, and he accordingly founded the Académie Royale de Danse, the fore-runner of all ballet. His advisors, deprived of participating in the ever more difficult steps of the Court Dancing that was now in the hands of professional dancers, turned at least part of their attention to what was already popular in England, English Country Dancing.

Where Court Dancing was intended mainly—but not exclusively—for one couple at a time who had been rigorously trained in the elaborate footwork required, Country Dancing was for couples in groups of two or more, using simple steps to trace patterns and figures over the ground and interacting with the other dancers in the set. Melusine Wood traces the roots of English Country Dancing to troubadors who lived in Provence in the south of France and who were driven out by the savage massacres by the Pope's forces in their crusade against the Albigensian heresy, beginning in 1208. Many of these refugees found shelter in England, where the dance tradition they started was permitted to develop almost in isolation from the rest of the world. By the time of Henry VIII (1509-1547) some of the dances had taken on forms recognisable today, including Dargason, Half Hannikin and Sellenger's Round.

It is believed that Elizabeth was interested mainly in Court Dancing until 1591 when she visited Lord and Lady Montague at Cowdray House in Sussex and watched her hosts doing Country Dances with their tenants. From that moment on, Country Dancing appears frequently in the records of entertainments at court, and presumably some new Country Dances were composed to be used at court because in 1600 the Maids of Honour were reported to be dancing both "the old and the new country dances." The popularity of Country Dancing at court continued during the reigns of James I and Charles I and even through the supposedly austere Commonwealth. From at least 1471 onwards, records exist of Court and Country dances being done by the young gentlemen at the Inns of Court (in the United States, the closest counterpart to the Inns of Court would be a Law School), but no published directions for any dances in England exist from before 1651.

John Playford

In 1651, when Puritan power in England was at its height, publisher John Playford (1623-1686) issued *The English Dancing Master: or Plaine and easie Rules for the Dancing of Country Dances, with the Tune to each Dance.* It is important to note that Playford himself probably did not write any of the dances, but merely served as the publisher. Experts feel they can detect the writing styles of six or eight different contributors, some of whom were merely putting into print dances that had been around for years, while others may have composed dances specially for the book. A fair number of typographical errors have caused some confusion in interpreting the dance instructions, but for the most part they are remarkably clear. Playford's shop was next to the Temple Church at one of the Inns of Court, which meant that his dance books had a ready market in all the law students that had to pass by his door on their way to and from classes. The book, which contains 105 dances, was so popular that Playford brought out many subsequent editions with new (or newly-collected old) dances, and the series was continued by his heirs long after Playford's death. All editions after the first dropped the word "English" from the title and were called simply *The Dancing Master*. The editions were as follows: Second, 1652; Third, 1657; another (revised) Third, 1665; Fourth, 1670; Fifth, 1675; Sixth, 1679; Seventh, 1686; Eighth, 1690; Ninth, 1695; Ninth, Part II, 1696; Ninth, a different Part II, 1698; Tenth, 1698; Eleventh, 1701; Twelfth, 1703; Thirteenth, 1706; Fourteenth, 1709; Fifteenth, 1713; Sixteenth, 1716; Seventeenth, 1721; Eighteenth, ca. 1728; Volume II, First, ca. 1713; Volume II, Second, 1714; Volume II, Third, 1718-19; Volume II, Fourth, 1728; Volume III, First, 1719; Volume III, Second, ca. 1727. By this time, others were bringing out their own dance books, most notably Walsh's *Complete Country Dancing Master*, 1718, and succeeding years. Surprisingly, many dances that can be traced to the Elizabethan period turn up for the first time in print in the later editions of Playford, sometimes more than a century after the first recorded reference to the title.

The English Dancing Mafter:
OR,
Plaine and eafie Rules for the Dancing of Country Dances, with the Tune to each Dance.

LONDON,
Printed by *Thomas Harper,* and are to be fold by *John Playford,* at his Shop in the Inner
Temple neere the Church doore. 1651.

Many collections of dances were published in England, Ireland and even in America in the eighteenth century. No specific record exists of Country Dancing in the earliest American settlements at Roanoke Island, North Carolina (1585-1589) and Jamestown, Virginia (1607 onwards), although it is very likely that dancing was done at both places. In the 1630s, some renegades were accused of running a licentious settlement at Wollaston, Massachusetts called Merry Mount, about mid-way between those centers of rectitude, Boston and Plymouth; these jolly folk are known to have danced around a maypole before they were driven out by their starchy neighbors, but the names of their dances are not recorded.

The earliest dances in America that are mentioned by name were done at a party called a Turtle Frolic* at Newport, Rhode Island on 23 December, 1752; these were "Arcadian Nuptials," "the Faithful Shepherd" (which first appeared in London about 1730) and "Peas Straw." Many years earlier in 1716, Edward Enstone, the organist at King's Chapel in Boston, announced that he would teach dancing, but there is no record of what dances he taught. Even earlier, Henri Sherlot, dancing master and perhaps a Huguenot refugee, was banished from Boston in 1681.

The history of Country Dance is closely related to the development of its physical formations, as society viewed the function of Country Dance in different ways. The earliest Country Dances called for three basic types of sets: a single line longways, a circle for as many as will and a double circle for as many as will. When, at some point in the sixteenth century, the gentry and nobility adopted Country Dance, many new forms were added, suitable for dancing in relatively small rooms; dancing had been moved inside the house. These new forms included square sets

---

* Frolic is an old word for dance; this one was named for a turtle because the dancers drank turtle soup at the party. Jim Morrison traces the description of this Turtle Frolic no further back than a nineteenth-century account, but there is no reason to suppose that it was not accurately quoting a lost original from the eighteenth century.

for two couples at a time, circles for three couples, double-line longways for three couples, squares and circles for four couples, double-line longways for four couples, and duple-minor double-line longways sets for as many as will, the latter especially suited to large houses with long picture-galleries.*

By the eighteenth century, several changes appeared. Completing the gentrification of Country Dancing, where instructions had once been for "Men" and "Women," the Georgian dance books were written for "Gentlemen" and "Ladies." By the beginning of the eighteenth century, the great variety of early formations had died away to two old ones, the duple-minor double-line progressive longways for as many as will and occasionally the three-couple longways set, plus a newcomer, the triple-minor double-line progressive longways for as many as will. Variety was offered by immigrant French dancing-masters who tried with only limited success to introduce so-called baroque and French court dance steps, such as the minuet step and the contretemps, descendants of the Court Dances of the previous century. Perhaps the instructors felt that exotic steps were the best way to ensure that they would have relatively steady employment, but what little evidence there is shows that the majority of dancers preferred to continue with the regular, simple Country Dance steps, the walking, running, slipping and skipping steps that remain popular today.

The French were, however, responsible for part of an important development that may have come directly across the Atlantic rather than via England. While the English had abandoned most of the many dance formations known in the England of 1600, the French continued to nurture the square formations for four couples that they had picked up from the English in the mid-seventeenth century. The French called these dances Cotillons, which was anglicized to Cotillions. They consisted of any of over a dozen well-known verses or "changes" each followed by a chorus or "figure" that was peculiar to that particular dance. Cotillions arrived in America with Rochambeau's troops at Newport, RI in 1780 (if not earlier) and remained popular for decades. A similar dance was called the Quadrille in the nineteenth century.

Folklorist Cecil Sharp and other commentators have noticed a decline in quality of the average written country dance dating from Playford's lifetime, and the decline was especially marked in the early nineteenth century. At the same time, Country Dances seemed to lose their appeal with the upper classes in the face of a challenge from new couple-dances, such as the Viennese waltz and later the polka. By 1900, the only Country Dance still danced by the English upper classes was "Sir Roger de Coverley," which was used to close the evening, and in America a similar dance of nineteenth-century origin, the "Virginia Reel," filled the same need; both are variations of the Elizabethan Country Dance "Trenchmore."

But Country Dancing was alive outside the upper classes. In England the country folk continued the form, although nearly all of their actual dances were of recent composition. In America, Country Dances had accompanied the settlers on their expansion to the west, but these settlers had left behind both dancing-masters and dance books, with a result that the dance forms underwent considerable change over the years. In the relatively remote communities of New England, like Vermont's Green Mountains, both square and longways formations survived, the latter under the name of Contras. When the French had first picked up English Country Dances, they called them "Contrée-Danses," using the French cognate word "Contrée," which later got shortened to "Contre" which sounded like "Contra" to the Americans. Although it would seem natural to call a dance that had lines of people opposite each other a "Contra" dance (after the Latin word "contra" meaning "against"), that was not the way in which the word developed, contrary to what contradancers often say.

Further west, only the square formations survived, but so transformed as to be scarcely recognisable: apart from the addition of newly-invented figures, western square dances depend entirely on a caller for instructions, and the figures are not necessarily danced to the phrases of the music. The new square dance form, however, did have enough power to spread around the globe; the irony was completed during and just after World War II when the then Princess Elizabeth actively encouraged the English to pick up the western square dance newly imported to England by American troops.

At the end of the nineteenth century a remarkable movement began that is still developing today, a movement that can best be called a revival, for it was concerned with reviving historical forms of folk-song, country dancing, musical instruments and ancient music to be played on if not ancient instruments at least instruments made and played according to ancient principles. Possibly the first of these revivalists was Arnold Dolmetsch, who, at about the same time as he had been appointed to teach violin at the Royal Academy of Music in the 1880s, discovered and bought a recorder and a rebec, two instruments that had been completely forgotten by his day. Dolmetsch soon began to make copies of these and many other early instruments, and much later his wife Mabel concerned herself with early dances and their music. Dolmetsch's work came to the attention of Ralph Vaughan-Williams and Cecil Sharp (1859-1924), and the latter was so taken with Country Dancing that he published six books of Country Dances early in the twentieth century containing a mixture of traditional dances he had observed in country villages

---

* Melusine Wood has discovered interesting parallels for many of these formations in fifteenth- and sixteenth-century Italy. Her work has been continued and clarified more recently by Julia Sutton, who has investigated the writings of Italian dancing-masters Negri and Caroso.

of England and America and other dances he had culled from various Playford editions.

The Sharp books have run through many reprints and have become the mainstay of dancing sponsored by the English Folk Dance & Song Society, the Country Dance & Song Society of America and many other groups around the world. Although he had more to go on than his counterparts to the north who were trying to reconstruct Scottish Country Dancing and although he was generally scrupulous in presenting and interpreting his material, Sharp encountered occasions where he was forced to guess what was intended by a term in Playford, and subsequent research by Sharp himself and by others, including Patrick Shuldham-Shaw, has proved that he sometimes guessed wrong.

At the time that Sharp first issued his books, many people in England, perhaps disillusioned with the heavy industrialization and materialism of the day, expressed a romantic nostalgia for the simpler life of Merrie England, which they felt could be recreated in part by reviving ancient folk traditions, such as fold-dancing on the village greens. Accordingly, Country Dancing experienced a tremendous revival for a short time, but the whole idea fell apart in the face of the onslaught of the First World War. After the war, Country Dancing was mostly limited to the school systems, where it stayed until released by the next great folk revival following World War II.

Here a few words should be said about the music that accompanies Country Dancing. Unlike modern squares and contras, which can and do use almost any music to hand, historical country dances are generally danced to music that is specific to the particular dance; thus, for experienced dancers, the old axiom "The music will tell you what to do" can be accurate. On the other hand, even in Playford's day, an alternate tune was occasionally substituted, as in the case of "The Geud Man of Ballangigh," and Sharp and subsequent writers have done likewise.

Most of the tunes of Elizabethan Country Dances also had words. In many cases, song-tunes were borrowed for dance tunes (but generally played too fast for singing) and perhaps in other cases some dance tunes were later made into songs. The medieval troubadors are said to have sung to accompany their dances, rather than use instrumental accompaniment, and so the connection between songs and dance is very old. While these songs and tunes were popular in their day, only a few, such as "Greensleeves," are well known today. "Sellenger's Round" was clearly based on the great Palm Sunday hymn, "All glory, laud and honour," while "Dargason" was later developed into the eighteenth-century tune "The Irish Washerwoman." The familiar nursery-rhyme "Mistress Mary quite contrary" will surprise many when they find that its original words were intended as a political satire about Mary Queen of Scots rather than children's fare; its last line was the title of its tune, "Cuckolds all a-row."

Most of this music was written in the period that has been sometimes called the golden age of English music. That the age was golden is usually thought to be a reflection of the brilliance of England's many exquisite composers* during the reigns of Elizabeth and James I. However, few if any of the dance tunes can be connected with any of these composers, some of whom wrote numerous Court Dance tunes, and yet they are still, for the most part, tunes of outstanding merit. Their quality has frequently been recognized by the inclusion of many of these tunes in numerous recordings not intended for accompanying dancing. The author would not be surprised if many non-dancers acquired this book for its musical content alone.

Music for Country Dancing can be played on just about any kind of instruments; Cecil Sharp expected that his editions would be played on the piano, and many bands have been formed to play for Playford dances with some combination of piano, bass, violin, flute, clarinet, concertina, accordian, banjo, guitar, electric guitar and drums. On the other hand, some readers may be interested in recreating as closely as possible the sounds to which these dances were originally danced. In the simplest of settings, dances were accompanied by a solo violin or rebec or a pipe (not unlike the more modern pennywhistle) and drum-like tabor or a fife or a bagpipe; other solo instruments that could be used alone or in concert with others were the organ (one of the chief objections of Puritans to organs in church was that they were also used outside the church for dancing), the hammered dulcimer, various kinds of harpsichords such as virginals and spinets, the lute, mandolin and cittern (pear-shaped English guitar) and even the Irish harp. Much music of the period was played on consorts or families of instruments: a group of recorders or straight flutes would be appropriate, from sopranino down to bass recorder (the latter is affectionately known as a "honking bedpost" by some of its aficionados), or a consort of viols from treble to bass or double-bass, or a consort of reed instruments like the shawm, the krumhorn and the regal, or even a consort of trombone-like sackbuts.

---

* a partial list of these composers: Adrian Batten, ca. 1590-1630; John Bennett, ca. 1570-1614; William Brade, 1560-1630; John Bull, ca. 1563-1628; William Byrd, 1543-1623; Thomas Campion, 1567-1620; John Cooper/Coperario, ca. 1575-1626; Richard Dering, 1580-1630; John Dowland, 1563-1626; John Farmer (16th century); Giles Farnaby, 1556-1640; Richard Farrant, ca. 1530-1580; Orlando Gibbons, 1583-1625; Nathaniel Giles, ca. 1558-1633; John Hilton, d.1608; Anthony Holborne, d.1602; Robert Jones, ca. 1577-16??; John Johnson, ca. 1540-1595; Robert Johnson, 1583-1633; George Kirbye (16th century); Thomas Morley, 1557-1602; John Munday, 1563-1630; Richard Nicolson, ca. 1570-1639; Robert Parsons (16th century); Thomas Tallis, ca. 1505-1585; John Taverner, ca. 1495-1545; Thomas Tomkins, 1572-1656; Christopher Tye, ca. 1500-1572; Thomas Weelkes, 1575-1623; Robert White, ca. 1538-1574; Thomas Whythorne, ca. 1528-ca. 1595; John Wilbye, 1574-1638; Robert Wylkynson (16th century).

Elizabethan composers and musicians also enjoyed experimenting with the "broken consort," in which instruments from different consorts would be combined, as for example, a treble recorder with an alto shawm, a viola da gamba and a bass sackbut. In fact, as long as common sense should prevail, there would probably not be a "wrong" way to build a broken consort for dancing, provided that both melody and rhythm were both clear.

Usually, as here, only the melody line was written out and the other players were expected to be proficient enough to find notes appropriate to their parts or to improvise, somewhat in the manner of jazz musicians. Occasionally, the bass part was also written under the melody line, and even indifferent musicians were trained to know how to play their parts by making reference to the bass line for their improvisations.

Country Dancing was and is intended, above all, to be fun for the dancers. It can also be fun to watch, especially if the watchers can look down on the geometric figures woven by the dancers. Country Dancing is a particularly appropriate way to celebrate anniversaries of historical events, and no doubt crowds of spectators would enjoy watching Elizabethan Country Dances at ceremonies marking the 400th anniversary of the establishment of the Sir Walter Ralegh colonies in North Carolina, 1985-9, the 400th birthday of the defeat of the Spanish Armada in 1988, the 350th anniversary of the founding of Rhode Island in 1986, the same year as the 350th birthday of Harvard University, and other such events. Organizations sponsoring Shakespeare plays and festivals will find Country Dances appropriate, both on and off stage, as will historical societies as they try to interpret period buildings or furnishings.

Perhaps some of the spectators will thereby be encouraged to become dancers themselves and join the growing number of people around the world who enjoy dancing Country Dances.

The list of dances in this book is not intended to be exhaustive of all the Country Dances known from the Elizabethan era, but it offers a representative sampling that should satisfy the appetites of most dancers. Similarly, due to the difficulties of documenting things accurately some four centuries later, it may be that a few dances of the early seventeenth century have crept into the book, although it is probably safe to assume that most of these dances were known in the sixteenth century. The selection has been, of necessity, the result of subjective judgements when documentation was lacking, and, in the same way, the interpretations of the dances is often a personal interpretation, filling in the many gaps in the originals or trying to make sense of Playford's frequent typographical errors. Every effort has been made to be true to the apparent styles of dancing of the period while at the same time making the dances fun for twentieth-century dancers and audiences. Enjoy!

THE DANCES

Most of the dances in this book are taken from the various editions of Playford; in fact, the only dances not taken from Playford are the Farandole, Rogero, Noel, Hey de Gie and the five processional dances, and the latter are not always considered to be Country Dances at all but rather a variation of Court Dances. Different methods were used to determine which of Playford's dances were already old enough at the time of publication as to be likely to have been known in Elizabeth's reign; the method most often used was to look for the name of the dance among lists of dances and songs from Elizabethan documents, and Chappell's *Popular Music of the Olden Time* was invaluable for providing such documentation.

However, it should be understood that just because a certain dance was noted, say, in 1570 it does not necessarily follow that Playford's publication of a dance of the same name about a century later was the same dance, although in the case of this book the two dances are assumed to be one and the same until proven otherwise. Furthermore, there is no proof that a tune that was known in, say, 1568 was used as a dance tune at so early a date, although such assumptions are made in this book.

On the basis of such assumptions, it is possible to spot various characteristics shared by many of these dances that are only infrequently found in any other Playford dances. For example, one recurring pattern is for a dance to have three verses (up a double and back; siding; arming) each followed by the same chorus. This pattern is occasionally found in later dances, but it is a good indication of early date, and accordingly "Rufty Tufty," for example, has been included in this collection although no early references to the title have yet been found.

People of the twentieth century, with its instant, world-wide communications, expect a high degree of standardization in their institutions; western square dances, for example, are done according to the same rules around the world. It was not so with English Country Dancing in the sixteenth century. "Sellenger's Round" could be danced as a round dance for as many as will, or as a longways dance for three couples, depending on the whim of those organizing the dance; "Dargason" could be a single-line longways dance or a circle for as many as will, and "Half Hannikin" could be a double-line longways dance or still another circle for as many as will.

Similarly, all English Country Dancers today are taught to start with the right foot for moving forward a double, to set first to the right, to arm first with the right, and so forth, just as all soldiers start marching with the left foot. Military marching was apparently not standardized until the reign of Frederick the Great in the eighteenth century, and there are indications that different groups of dancers chose the right foot or the left foot mostly on a whimsical basis before about 1700; Playford's contributors even presented dances in which the women were on the left of their partners. The directions in this book have been standardized in accordance with what is normally done by Country Dancers around the world, but if a demonstration group were to show dances in which the left foot were favored it would not necessarily be wrong by Elizabethan standards; but then the Elizabethans could not get into a motorcar and be at a dance fifty miles away in less than an hour, so they had little need to standardize.

Some characteristics of English Country Dancing remain the same regardless of which dance is being considered. First, Country Dances are dances of interaction with other people, both partner and other couples. The interaction is shown through eye-contact between the various people doing a particular figure, and by exerting a reasonable amount of tension in the arms when holding hands with another dancer. Second, the types of steps normally done in Country Dancing are few in number and simple to execute; the most common is a simple walking step with a certain amount of spring in it and the dancer's weight well forward over the balls of the feet. The same weight-distribution should also be used for the skipping step (which surely need not be defined), the slipping or chassé step (a fast sideways movement) and the rarely-used skip-change step.

Third, Country Dances are danced, not unlike a military march in that regard, with each step falling on a beat of the music, and each figure generally corresponding to the phrases of the music, which are normally two, four or eight bars long with two steps to the bar (or occasionally three steps to the measure when the music calls for it).

Fourth, to a certain extent, Country Dances are usually directional. It is necessary to establish in which direction the "presence" is located, a term that referred to where royalty would be seated for watching the dancing, or, failing that, usually where the musicians or audience are situated; that direction is called "up" or above, while the opposite direction is obviously "down" or below.

Country Dances offer great variety of formations or "sets," which can be enjoyed merely for the sake of variety or for the often real problems of lack of space or shortage of dancers. The smallest sets are for only two couples at a time in a square formation with couple facing couple, the woman always being on her partner's right. The dancers closest to the presence are the number one man and the number two woman; they are "up."

Similar to the two-couple square is the three-couple circle, in which the couple nearest the presence is numbered one, the couple to their left, two, and the last couple, three (numbering clockwise). Another formation for three couples, however, is a longways set, in which the set is arranged in two columns facing eachother; viewed from the presence, the men's column would be on the right and the women's column on the left. The number one couple is at the top or closest to the presence and the other couples are numbered accordingly. When a dancer is on his or her own side, he is called "proper" but if he is on the women's side and vice versa, he is called "improper," two important terms.

Like the dances for three couples, dances for four couples have two different formations. The four-couple longways set is similar to the three-couple longways set with the addition of an extra couple at the bottom. The four-couple circle or square resembles the three-couple circle in that the woman is always on her partner's right, but terminology is changed. The couple nearest the presence is numbered one, with the numbering following around the set clockwise, but numbers one and three are also called "heads" while two and four are known as "sides," the origin of the square dance.

In larger circles for "as many as will," numbering is not normally needed, but the woman is still on the right of her partner. For processional double circles, the men may form the outer ring while the women may form the inner ring, and both rings normally face clockwise; this is at odds with the findings of Renaissance-dance scholar Patri Pugliese, but it means that the man with his longer legs will be better able to cover the longer distance around the outer circle than the woman, while at the same time he keeps his partner on his right so she does not trip on the sword he may sometimes be wearing at his left side.

The last formation to be mentioned is the longways double-column for as many as will. This is the most popular of all Country Dance sets, but the most difficult to describe on paper. Like the longways dances for three and four couples, the men and women are formed into two facing columns (as a practical matter, it is best not to have more than ten couples in each set). The most important difference, however, in the longer dances is that they usually contain a progression in order to give all the couples an opportunity to take on the "active" role.

For a very few early dances, the progression is merely that the original top couple finds itself at the bottom of the set after going through the figures of the dance, leaving room for a new top couple to begin the figures. However, the more normal method of progression is obtained by dividing the set into "minor sets" of two couples at a time ("duple-minor") or, from the eighteenth-century onwards, many dances were divided into minor sets of three couples at a time ("triple-minor"). Thus, in a duple-minor, every other couple is a number one or "active," starting with the top couple, and the couple below each number one is a two or "inactive." At the end of each round of dance figures, all the ones will have progressed one place down the set while all the twos progress one place up the set. When a one gets to the bottom or a two gets to the top, it waits out for one round of the dance and then rejoins the dance as the opposite number from what it had before. In a triple-minor dance, the progression is slightly more complicated, for, although the ones remain ones all the way to the bottom, the other dancers switch back and forth between being twos and threes until they reach the top, at which point they have to wait out two turns before resuming the dance as ones.

There remain a few points of terminology and style before the dance figures are examined. The identification of one's partner is obvious, but certain other people are called opposites, corners and contraries. In a round or square set, a man's corner is the woman to his left, while a woman's corner is the man to her right. In a duple-minor longways, 1 Man and 2 Woman are first corners, and 2 Man and 1 Woman are second corners. In a square set, one's opposite is the person of the opposite sex directly across the set. In a longways set for three couples or in triple-minor form, the person in number two position looks across the set to the right to see the first contrary and across the set to the left to see the second contrary; "contrary" is short for "contrary corner."

Country Dancing depends to a certain extent on proper use of hands and arms. When dancers take hands for a turn or a star, they should use a normal hand-shake grip, and not any specialized wrist or thumb grip invented in more recent times. The hands should be slightly below the elbows, which in turn should be below the shoulders; the arms should form a catenary curve under tension from the shoulder of the one dancer to the shoulder of the other. In a turn or a star, each dancer should lean slightly outwards to keep the tension, but when slipping around in a ring, strangely enough, the dancers should lean slightly forward to maintain the correct tension and keep the circle round.

All Country Dances should begin and end with Honours to one's partner. Many musical groups, both live and recorded, neglect to give the important music at the beginning for bows and courtesies (curtsy is a contraction of courtesy), a practice that is to be deplored. Various different ways of honouring have been used over the years, but one particular way seems to have been popular from the sixteenth through the eighteenth centuries. The man places his right foot back about a foot behind his left and pointing at right angles to it. He then bends his right knee but keeps his left leg straight and his waist almost straight, and gazes at his partner. The woman keeps both feet together at a 45-degree angle, or she may place her left foot ever so slightly behind the right, and, bending her knees outwards but not her waist, gracefully sinks and rises again, her glance slightly downcast.

Since Country Dancing is danced to the phrase of the music, which is normally in four, eight or sixteen counts, the dance steps are arranged to fit such music. The "single" step is actually two steps, the first in whichever direction specified by one foot, and the second to bring the other foot up to the first foot in closed position. The "double" step is actually four steps, bringing the trailing foot up to the other foot on the fourth count. Two doubles means a total of eight steps with the trailing foot coming up to the other foot on the eighth beat and sometimes on the fourth beat as well; two doubles are often used when slipping left or right around a circle, in which case the dancer lands on both feet together on the eighth count. An instruction frequently encountered is "up a double and back," which means to go forward a double, starting on the right foot, and when that is completed go backwards a double.

Explanations of many Country Dance figures follow below in alphabetical order.

Allemand—see Turn

Arming

Two different ways of arming are currently done, and both appear to be historically accurate. The simpler version, and probably the more rustic, is for the two dancers to link elbows (right elbows for "Arm Right" and left elbows for "Arm Left") and walk forwards around in a circle once, ending back in original places. The alternative way is for the couple to hold eachother by a forearm grip with the man's hand under and supporting the woman's elbow.

Back to Back

In this figure, which is also called Dos-à-dos or do-si-do, two dancers face eachother, move forward and pass eachother by right shoulders; then, each one moves slightly to his right and dances backwards back to original place, having passed the other dancer by left shoulders on the way back. Dancers continue facing in the same direction throughout the figure.

Casting

Casting is a movement that begins by turning to face the direction opposite to that in which one wishes to go before continuing to turn to face the desired direction. For example, in the most commonly-found situation, a man in a longways set "casts off" (down) into the second place by turning to his left to face up, then out and then down. When he arrives in second place, he will have traced a spiral shape on the floor. In casting up, he would turn to face down first. In a longways set, every time the 1s cast, the 2s should move up into the 1s' place, usually on beats 5, 6, 7 and 8.

Change Places

Two dancers change places (usually the instructions are directed at corners) by passing by right shoulders unless otherwise directed. Passing by right shoulders is probably derived from the English custom of passing on foot or on horseback by right shoulders (and now in motorcars in England) so as to give one a chance to draw the sword out of the sheath on the left side to defend oneself if necessary. When corners cross or change places, unless directions say otherwise, the First Corners (first man and second woman) change first.

Circle

Three or more dancers take hands in a ring, their arms in a catenary curve, and dance around the ring clockwise unless instructed otherwise. The normal step for this is the walking step, but on many occasions the slipping step is more appropriate.

Cross Over One Couple

In a longways set, the top couple of each minor set crosses over by right shoulders and goes into the second place, improper, while the 2s move up. The figure may or may not end with the couple crossing back to their own side again, sometimes giving two hands as they go.

Dos-à-Dos—see Back to Back

Figure-8 and Half Figure-8

In a figure-8, a dancer will trace a figure-8 on the floor by weaving a path around two other stationary dancers. In a longways set, the couple will cross, the man allowing the woman to go in front of him each time they meet, the man going first around the woman of the stationary couple while the woman goes around the stationary man; then the man goes around the stationary man while the woman goes around the stationary woman until both dancers are back in places. In a half figure-8, only the first part of the figure-8 is done, which leaves the dancers improper.

Gypsy

In a gypsy (also known colloquially as a gip), two dancers move around eachother clockwise in eight counts without touching, but almost as if they were doing a right-hand turn. In most gypsies, the dancers face eachother throughout the figure, but occasionally instructions tell the dancers to face outwards instead.

Hands Across—see Star

Hey

Heys abound in great variety, but essentially they are weaving figures in which usually everyone moves, unlike the figure-8 in which the weaving is done around a stationary couple. In a circular hey (always done with an even number of poeple, whether four or as many as will), partners face and pass eachother by right shoulders, and then pass the next person by the left, and so forth, alternating between right and left shoulders until the end of the figure. Occasionally, directions will call for just two or three changes of a circular hey when two couples are doing the figure. When dancers take hands as they pass, first right hands then left hands, the figure is known as "Rights and Lefts" or simply "Right and Left." If the Rights and Lefts are for more than two couples, the figure is known as a "Grand Chain," from the French "la grande chaine."

In a longways major or minor set for three couples, a straight hey for three is done by the top person facing down and all others facing up, so the 1s can pass the 2s by right shoulders and the 3s by left shoulders. At the bottom, the dancer continues turning left until he is again facing the 2, whom he passes by the left and once more the 3 whom he passes by the right until he is home again. All dancers reaching the bottom turn to the left, while all dancers reaching the top turn to the right, and all follow the same track.

When straight heys for three are being done simultaneously in both lines, they should often be mirror heys. In a mirror hey, the men do exactly what they normally do in a straight hey, but the women do a mirror image of the men's figure; the first woman starts by passing the second woman by the left shoulder. Dancers reaching top or bottom should take hands briefly with their partners. A useful mnemonic device for mirror heys is the expression "middles bulge," for the couple in the middle is always dancing towards the outside.

A more complicated version of mirror heys is "hey on the opposite side." While the other dancers do a normal mirror hey, the top couple cross over heading down the set, the woman going in front of the man, and go out between the 2s and 3s on the improper side. They continue the hey as if they were part of that side until they reach the top. At this point, they again cross over as they head down the set and go out between the 2s and 3s on their proper sides, while the 2s and 3s do a second mirror hey in the normal way.

Some eighteenth-century dances employ a Scottish figure, a straight hey for four (the Scots actually call them reels); the dancers on the ends face inwards and those on the inside face outwards. As they go in *and* out of the ends, they pass by right shoulders, and as they go through the middle they pass by left shoulders. This same system can be expanded to form a straight hey for any even number of dancers, as long as they are arranged so as to face eachother in couples.

Finally, progressive heys occasionally appear in longways dances. The top couple faces and starts the hey passing by the right, while all the rest of the dancers face up and wait until the active dancers reach them before taking part in the hey, which ends when everyone is back home.

Lead out the Sides

In a three-couple or triple-minor longways dance, the couple then in the middle (usually the 1s who have moved into middle position) lead out between the two other women, separate, go around the top and bottom of the set respectively, meet in the middle and lead out between the two other men. Separate again, go around the top and bottom of the set again and return to middle places. The man is usually above the woman during this weaving figure reminiscent of the figure-8.

Poussette and Half-Poussette

Partners take both hands. The upper man pushes his partner towards the wall on the women's side while the lower man pulls his partner towards the men's wall until they are clear of eachother. At this point the upper couple maneuvers slightly down the set while the other couple maneuvers up the set and they push or pull back into the lines in progressed places. Thus far, the figure is called a half-poussette. A whole poussette is simply the continuation of this process back to original places. A poussette is, in effect, for couples what the back-to-back is for individuals. It is nearly always clockwise, although one nineteenth-century dance book suggests that a poussette should be counter-clockwise. The word comes from the French verb "pousser," meaning to push, and the instruction to push is presumed always to be given to the man in first position.

Rights and Lefts—see Hey

Setting

In its most common form, the setting step is no more than a Single to the right followed by a Single to the left (step to the right and close, step to the left and close). Very often, setting is done by partners to eachother, which means, first of all, that one zigs when the other zags (if they are both going to the right, they are going in opposite directions), and second, that partners should take advantage of this opportunity to interact with eachother by setting not quite to the side but slightly forward towards eachother; in such cases, setting is often followed by Turn Single, which enables them to get back into lines again.

The setting step has traditionally afforded dancers the greatest opportunity for individualism; we read about sailors, for example, who would spend off-watch hours "footing it" or setting to partners on the foredeck of the ship, presumably trying to invent ever more impressive variations. Among the variations more often used are the Scottish Pas de Basque, a simplified Pas de Basque without the kick at the end of each half, the Rigadoon, the Beaton step, and the half-Althea kicking set, which, although Elizabethan in origin, has been adopted by New England contra-dancers as "Balance."

A variation of the setting step that is required in some early dances is called "slow set and honour." In this, each half of the setting is punctuated by a brief honour, thus: step to the right and honour, step to the left and honour.

Siding

Playford never described in detail what was meant by the instruction to side. Sharp therefore invented a figure that filled the required number of bars of music and looked elegant, and indeed the Sharp siding has proved to be enduringly popular. However, Sharp himself discovered early eighteenth-century descriptions of siding that were quite different from his own (as he admitted in the introduction to *The Country Dance Book*, vol. VI, pp. 10 and 11), but he hesitated to urge dancers to change, presumably since his own invention by that time was so widely used. Patrick Shuldham-Shaw lacked Sharp's hesitation and urged dancers to adopt the original type of siding, with the result that the original siding is often called "Shaw siding," or simply "side-by-side." The author submits that the Sharp siding is no longer appropriate for historical dances, although it is elegant enough to be continued in use in dances of recent composition if desired.

In the original siding, the two dancers advance a double (using small steps) towards eachother so that they end up in a line beside eachother, right shoulder to right shoulder, and then retire back to places. The second time, the dancers advance left shoulder to left shoulder and retire.

Since many dance groups still insist on the Sharp siding, it may be useful to describe it here: starting with the right foot, dancers advance a double, passing eachother by the left shoulder and turning to face eachother as they go; then, retrace steps back to places (which results in the dancers actually passing eachother by the right shoulder before turning to face eachother).

Star

The star, or "hands across," as it is called in historical dance books, is usually danced by four people. Dancers reach into the middle with right hands and take the hand of the dancer diagonally across from them in a handshake grip; the hands should be slightly below the shoulders, and the arms should be under reasonable tension. The dancers then move the star around clockwise back to places, or occasionally only half way around. A right hand star is often followed by a left-hand star, which rotates counter-clockwise. No fancy thumb or wrist grips should be used in historical dances.

Turn

As in a star, two dancers take right hands as if about to shake hands, making sure that the hands are below the shoulders and that the arms are under reasonable tension, and turn eachother once around clockwise back to places. Sometimes, a turn can be required to be half, three-quarters, once-and-a-quarter or once-and-a-half around. The same instructions apply to a left-hand turn, exept that the dancers rotate counter-clockwise. In a two-hand turn, the man's hands support the woman's, and the turn is always done clockwise.

In the eighteenth century, a figure related to the turn, known as the Allemand, became popular. Dancers place their arms as if they were about to arm by the right, but with their left hands they reach behind their own backs to grasp the other dancer's right hand. They then go once around clockwise. The Allemand Reverse is similar, but done with left arms and counter-clockwise.

Turn Single

In spite of its name, the turn single involves a double step. The word "single" merely instructs the dancer to turn alone. This is not a spin around on one foot, but it is as if one were walking around the outside of an LP record lying on the floor. The turn single is usually to the right or clockwise, but there are occasions when turning to the left is indicated; one such occasion is sometimes described as a "cloverleaf turn single," in which the first woman and the second man turn to the right and the first man and the second woman turn to the left. The turn single can also be used as a travelling step for short distances; for example, if it follows, as if often does, setting to partner, the dancers will probably have moved slightly forward out of line, and the turn single can bring them back into lines.

We are frolic here in Court; much dancing in the Privy Chamber of Country Dances before the Queen's Majesty, who is exceedingly pleased therewith.

> Letter from the Earl of Worcester to the Earl of Shrewsbury, 1602, quoted in Chappell, p. 626

For what clipping, what culling, what kissing and bussing, what smooching and slavering one of another, what filthie groping and uncleane handling is not practised in those dancings?

> Philip Stubbs, *Anatomy of Abuses*, 1583

Everie shipe caries cannon and . . . dromes, trompetts, taber, pipe, and other instruments. . . .

> Sir Jerome Horsey's dialogue with Tsar Ivan IV, 1576, quoted in *Russia at the Close of the Sixteenth Century*, Hakluyt Society, 1856, pp. 185-6

. . . with the sound of trumpets, and a consort of musick

> description of Sir Richard Grenville's banquet for Spanish officials in Hispaniola, 1585, quoted in Hakluyt, *Principal Navigations*, 1589, p. 735.

. . . in his Pinnesse with his musike, and trumpets, and I in my skiffe with trumpets, drum and fife, and tabor, and pipe, accompanied them.

> Luke Ward's description of entertaining Portuguese officials on the coast of Brazil, quoted *Ibid.*, p. 666.

. . . or do as Dick Harvey did, that having preacht and beat downe three pulpits in inveighing against dauncing, one Sunday evening, when his wench or friskin was footing it aloft on the greene, with foote out and foote in, . . . he came sneaking behind a tree, and lookt on; and though hee was loth to be seen to countenance the sport, having God's word against it so dreadfully; yet to shew his good will to it in heart, hee sent her eighteen pence in huggermugger (ie., secretly), to pay the fiddlers.

> Nashe, *Have with You to Saffron Walden*, 1596, as quoted in Chappell, p. 116.

THOMAS NASHE, 1597

A Treatise of Daunces, wherein it shewed, that they are as it were accessories and dependants (or things annexed) to whoredom. Where also by the way is touched and proved, that playes are joyned and knit together in a rancke or rowe with them.

> Title page of a tract at Lambeth Palace Library, 1590, no. 37.

But wee now in Christian countries have schools of dauncing, howbeit that it is no wonder, seeing also we have houses of baudrie. . . . it is well knowne, that by daunces, and leapings very many honest marriages are brought to passe, and, therefore it is good and tolerable.

> The Rev. John Northbrooke, *A Treatise Against Dicing, Dancing, Plays, and Interludes, with Other Idle Pastimes*, 1577, reprinted for the Shakespeare Society, 1843, pp. 159, 166.

But I should like to have acquired skill in dancing; . . . I much enjoy fencing and tennis and this placed me on friendly terms with young men, but without a knowledge of dancing I could not please the damsels, upon whom it seems to me the entire reputation of an eligible young man depends. . . . If you desire to marry, you must realise that a mistress is won by good temper and grace displayed while dancing, because ladies do not like to be present at fencing or tennis, lest a splintered sword or a blow from a tennis ball should cause them injury. . . . And there is more to it than this, for dancing is practised to reveal whether lovers are in good health and sound of limb, after which they are permitted to kiss their mistresses in order that they may touch and savour one another, thus to ascertain if they are shapely or emit an unpleasant odour as of bad meat. Therefore, from this standpoint, quite apart from the many other advantages to be derived from dancing, it becomes essential in a well-ordered society.

> T. Arbeau, *Orchesographie*, 1588, New York, 1967, p. 12

Dancing is for the most part attended with many amorous smiles, wanton compliments, unchaste kisses, scurrilous songs & sonnets, effeminate music, lust-provoking attire, ridiculous love-pranks, all which savour only of sensuality, of raging fleshly lusts. Therefore, it is wholly to be abandoned of all good Christians. Dancing serves no necessary use, no profitable, laudable or pious end at all. It issues only from the inbred pravity, vanity, wantonness, incontinency, pride, profaneness or madness of men's depraved natures. Therefore, it must needs be unlawful unto Christians. The way to Heaven is too steep, too narrow for men to dance and keep revel rout. No way is large or smooth enough for capering roysters, for jumping, skipping, dancing dames but that broad, beaten, pleasant road that leads to hell. The gate of Heaven is too narrow for whole rounds, whole troops of dancers to march in together.

> William Prynne, *Histriomastix*, as quoted on *The Compleat Dancing Master*, Island Records, 1974.

He hath no pleasure in the strength of an horse, neither delighteth He in any man's legs.

> Psalm 147, v. 10, Coverdale translation, 1546.

Let them praise His Name in the dance.

> Psalm 149, v. 3, Coverdale translation, 1546.

Praise Him in the timbrels and dances.

> Psalm 150, v. 4, Coverdale translation, 1546.

Sir Richard Champernown, to whom Anthony Holborne dedicated the publishing of his musical collection in 1599, had a particularly fine band of musicians, which caused the family's ruin. "For that Mr. Champernown, taking it on the Thames in the time of Queen Elizabeth, her Majesty was so delighted with the music that she requested the loan of it for a month: to which Mr. Champernown, aware of the improbability of its ever returning, would not consent, saying that he hoped her Majesty would allow him to keep his fancy. The Queen was so highly exasperated at his refusal that she found some pretence to sue him at law and ruin him, by obliging him, in the course of the proceedings, to sell no fewer than 18 manors."

> J. Britton & E. W. Braylay, *The Beauties of England & Wales*, 1803, as quoted by Christopher Ball on Musical Heritage Society 3602.

The art of Dancing . . . is a commendable and rare Quality fit for yong Gentlemen, if opportunely and civilly used. (Dancing is) Excellent for Recreation, after more serious Studies, making the body active and strong, gracefull in deportment, and a quality very much beseeming a Gentleman.

> J. Playford, *The English Dancing Master*, 1651 (introduction).

Her Majestie that Saturday night was lodg'd in the Castell of Warwick; where she restid all Sonday, where it pleased her to have the country people, resorting to see her, daunce in the Court of the Castell, her Majestie beholding them out of her chamber window; which thing, as it pleas'd well the country people, so it seemed her Majesty was much delighted, and made very myrry.

> Sixteenth-century journal entry quoted in Nichol's *Progresses*, 1823, Vol. I, p. 319.

Now, gallants, while the town-musicians finger their frets within; and the mad lads and country lasses, every mother's child, with nosegays and bride-laces in their hats, dance all their country measures, rounds and jigs, what shall we do? Hark! They're all on the Hey; they toil like mill-horses, and turn as round; marry, not on the toe: aye, and they caper, but not without cutting; you shall see tomorrow the hall floor peck'd and dinted like a mill-stone, made with their high shoes: though their skill be small, yet they tread heavy where their hob-nails fall.

> Thomas Heywood, *A Woman Kill'd with Kindness*, 1600.

The man that hath no music in himself,
Nor is not mov'd with concord of sweet sounds,
Is fit for treasons, stratagems, and spoils;
The motions of his spirit are as dull as night,
And his affections dark as Erebus.
Let no such men be trusted. Mark the Music.

> William Shakespeare

SOME EARLY REFERENCES TO SPECIFIC DANCES IN LITERATURE

John Skelton, *Against Venomous Tongues*, 1529:
> Hey de Gie.

Feuillerat, *Revels of Edward VI*, 1551:
> Trenchmore

Rychardes(?), *Misogonus*, ca. 1560:
> The Catching of Quails, Heartsease, Putney Ferry, The Shaking of the Sheets, The Vicar of Saint Fools.

William Bulleyn, *A Dialogue both Pleasaunte and Pietifull*, 1564:
> Hey de Gie, Trenchmore.

Nicholas Breton, *Works of a Young Wit*, 1577:
> All Flowers of the Broom, Hey de Gie, The Lusty Gallant (Fain I Would).

Edmund Spenser, *The Shepheardes Calender*, 1579:
> Hey de Gie.

Stephen Gosson, *School of Abuse*, 1579:
> Rogero, The Shaking of the Sheets, Trenchmore, Turkeloney.

William Webbe, *Discourse of English Poetrie*, 1586:
> Downright Squire, Rogero, Trenchmore.

Thomas Nashe & Philip Sidney, *Astrophel and Stella*, 1591:
> Trip and Go (The Boatman).

"Philip Foulface," *Bacchus' Bountie*, 1593:
> Sellenger's Round.

Thomas Nashe, *The Terrors of the Night*, 1594:
> The Lusty Gallant (Fain I Would).

Thomas Nashe, *Have with You to Saffron-Waldon*, 1596:
> All Flowers of the Broom, Basilino, Greensleeves, Half Hannikin, Peggy Ramsey, Peppers Black, Rogero, Turkeloney.

William Shakespeare, *Romeo & Juliet*, 1597:
> Heartsease.

Deloney, *History of the Gentle Craft*, 1598:
> Trenchmore.

Thomas Dekker, *The Shoemaker's Holiday*, 1600:
> Rogero.

Thomas Heywood, *A Woman Killed with Kindness*, 1600:
> The Beginning of the World (Sellenger's Round), The Cushion Dance, The Hunting of the Fox (Trenchmore), John, Come Kiss Me Now, Put on Thy Smock a Monday, Rogero, The Shaking of the Sheets, Tom Tiler.

Thomas Middleton, *Father Hubburd's Tales*, 1604
> Sellenger's Round.

'Tis Merry When Gossips Meet, 1609:
> John, Come Kiss Me Now.

John Fletcher, *Love's Cure*, ca. 1615.
> Put on Thy Smock a Monday.

A Navy of Land Ships, 1627:
> Trenchmore.

Thomas Heywood, *Fair Maid of the West*, 1631:
> Sellenger's Round, Tom Tiler.

Ben Jonson, *Tale of a Tub*, 1633:
> Dargason, The Jolly Joiner, The Jovial Tinker (Under & Over), Tom Tiler

All in a Garden Green HM 1039
Althea PLA2
The Beggar Boy CDS8 ARA6520
The Black Nag CDS6
The Boatman PLA3 CDS8 ARA6520
Broom, the Broom, the Bonny, Bonny Broom PLA2
Chestnut PLA1 ARA6520
Cuckolds All A-Row PLA1 HELP17 HM1039
Dargason PLA1 ARA6520
Dissembling Love PLA4 ARA6520
Drive the Cold Winter Away HM1109
Epping Forest PLA4 CDS7
Fain I Would PLA2
The Fine Companion CDS9 ARA6520 HM1109
The Frair and the Nun PLA2 HM1109
Gathering Peascods PLA1 CDS9 ARA6520
The Geud Man of Ballangigh (Hunt the Squirrel) PLA4 cds6
Greensleeves LIB3 CDS8 HM1039
Grimstock PLA1 HM1109
Half Hannikin HM1109
Heartsease PLA3 CDS8 ARA6520
Hit and Miss PLA3 CDS7
Hyde Park HM1039
Jenny Pluck Pears PLA1 ARA6520 HM1109
Jog On HM1039
Lavena (for Picking Up Sticks) PLA3 CDS7 ARA6520
Mad Robin CDS7
Mage on a Cree PLA1
The Maid in the Moon PLA4 CDS8
The Maid Peept out at the Window VAR013 ARA6520
Maiden Lane PLA2 VAR013 HM1039
The Merry, Merry Milkmaids PLA2 ARA6520 HM1039
Newcastle ARA6520 HM1039
Nightpiece PLA4
Nobody's Jig PLA3 LIB3
Paul's Steeple HM1109
Paul's Wharf HM1039
The Queen's Jig (late tune) PLA4 CDS7
Rufty Tufty CDS6 ARA6520 HM1109
Scotch Cap CDS7
Sellenger's Round PLA3 CDS6 HELP17
Shepherd's Holiday CDS8
Stanes Morris ARA6520
Upon a Summer's Day PLA1 CDS9 ARA6520 HM1109
Woody Cock ARA6520 HM1039

Select Discography—only Long-Playing Records

1 *The English Dancing Master I* (14 Playford dances) EFDSS PLA 1
2 *The English Dancing Master II* (14 Playford dances) EFDSS PLA 2
3 *The English Dancing Master III* (13 Playford Dances) EFDSS PLA 3
4 *The English Dancing Master IV* (13 Playford Dances) EFDSS PLA 4
5 *Country Dances, New Series* (11 dances, mostly Playford) EFDSS LIB 3
6 *The Compleat Dancing Master* (15 dances, many Playford) (British) Island Records HELP 17
7 *By Popular Demand* (13 dances, mostly Playford) CDS 6
8 *Popular English Country Dances of the 17th and 18th Centuries* (13 dances, mostly Playford) CDS 7
9 *Step Stately* (16 dances, mostly Playford) CDS 8
10 *Juice of Barley—Simple English Country Dances* (13 dances, 7 from Playford) CDS 9
11 *Bare Necessities* (11 dances, mostly Playford) Varrick Records V 013
12 *Popular Tunes in 17th Century England—The Broadside Band* (12 Playford Dances, plus others) Harmonia Mundi (France) HM 1039
13 *Country Dances—The Broadside Band* (19 Playford Dances) Harmonia Mundi (France) HM 1109
14 *Country Capers* (25 Playford Dances) Arabesque 6520

All the EFDSS, CDS and Varrick records are available from the Country Dance and Song Society,
505 Eighth Avenue
New York, NY, 10018

All the EFDSS records and some of the others are available from the English Folk Dance and Song Society,
Cecil Sharp House,
2 Regent's Park Road,
London, NW1 7AY

Some of the books in the bibliography are also available from both these addresses.

A Select Bibliography

Thoinot Arbeau, *Orchesographie*, Langres, 1589; reprint of translation, New York, 1967.
William Chappell, *Popular Music of the Olden Time*, 2 volumes, London, 1859, facsimile reprint, New York, 1965.
James P. Cunningham, *Dancing in the Inns of Court*, London, 1965.
Mabel Dolmetsch, *Dances of England and France from 1450 to 1600*, London, 1949.
George S. Emmerson, *A Social History of Scottish Dance*, London, 1972.
John Forrest, *Morris and Matachin*, Sheffield, 1984.
Douglas and Helen Kennedy, *Country Dance Book New Series*, London, 1979.
Priscilla and Robert Lobley, *Your Book of English Country Dancing*, London, 1980.
John Playford, *The English Dancing Master*, London, 1651, facsimile edition, London 1957.
John Playford, *The English Dancing Master*, London, 1651, revised edition, London, 1933; paperback, New York, 1975.
Patri J. Pugliese and Joseph Casazza, *Practise for Dauncing*, Cambridge, Massachusetts, 1980.
Guido Sarducci, "Discovery of a New Mode in Modal Music: the Pyala," *L'Osservatore Romano*, Rome, 1 April, 1984 (special edition).
Cecil J. Sharp, *The Country Dance Book*, parts I-VI, London, 1909ff, reprinted and revised in 3 volumes, London, 1975.
Cecil J. Sharp, *Country Dance Tunes*, London, 1911ff, reprinted London, 1976.
Frank C. Van Cleef, *Twenty Four Country Dances from the Playford Editions*, West Hartford, Connecticut, 1979.
Melusine Wood, *Historical Dances (Twelfth to Nineteenth Century)*, London, 1964.
Melusine Wood, "Some Notes on the English Country Dance before Playford," *English Folk Dance and Song Society Journal*, London, Dec. 1937.

Thanks are due to the EFDSS Library in London, Kate Van Winkle Keller, Gail & Leland Ticknor and my patient wife Cathy.

A LIST OF THE DANCES

Two-Couple Square Set (6)
1 Althea
2 Cuckolds All A-row
3 Heartsease
4 Hit and Miss
5 Rogero
6 Rufty Tufty

Three-Couple Circular Set (6)
7 The Gelding of the Devil
8 Greenwood
9 Jenny Pluck Pears
10 The Maid in the Moon
11 Put on Thy Smock a Monday
12 Putney Ferry

Three-Couple Longways Set (16)
13 All in a Garden Green
14 The Beggar Boy/Lucina
15 The Black Nag
16 The Boatman/Trip and Go
17 Chestnut/Dove's Figary
18 Dissembling Love/The Lost Heart
19 Greensleeves
20 Grimstock
21 Maiden Lane
22 Picking of Sticks (original tune)
23 Scotch Cap
24 The Shaking of the Sheets/Nightpiece
25 Shepherd's Holiday/Labour in Vain
26 Upon a Summer's Day
27 The Whish
28 Woody Cock

Four-Couple Longways Set (11)
29 Broom, the Broom, the Bonny, Bonny Broom
30 Cherrily and Merrily
31 Daphne
32 Goddesses/Quodling's Delight
33 Lady Spellor
34 The maid Peept out at the Window/The Friar in the Well
35 Mall Peatley
36 The Merry, Merry Milkmaids
37 Milkmaids' Bob
38 The Shepherd's Daughter
39 Ten Pound Lass

Four-Couple Square or Circular Set (16)
40 The Catching of Quails
41 Fain I Would/The Lusty Gallant
42 The Fine Companion
43 Hunsdon House
44 Hyde Park
45 If All the World Were Paper
46 Mage on a Cree
47 Millfield
48 Newcastle/Newcastle Old
49 Oaken Leaves
50 Oranges and Lemons
51 Peppers Black
52 Rose Is White and Rose Is Red
53 Sage Leaf
54 Up Tails All
55 Winifred's Knot/Open the Door to Three

Circular Set for as Many as Will (7)
56 Dargason/The Sedany
57 Epping Forest
58 Gathering Peascods
59 Half Hannikin
60 Hey de Gie
61 Noël
62 Sellenger's Round/The Beginning of the World

Non-progressive Longways Set for as Many as Will (2)
63 Drive the Cold Winter Away
64 The New Bo Peep/Pickadilla

Progressive Longways Set for as Many as Will (2)
65 Stanes Morris
66 Trenchmore/The Hunting of the Fox

Duple-Minor Progressive Longways Set for as Many as Will (14)
67 The Catching of Fleas
68 The Fit's upon Me Now
69 The Friar and the Nun
70 The Geud Man of Ballangigh/The Gaberlunzie Man (original tune)
71 Jog On
72 Lady, Lie near Me
73 Mad Robin
74 The New Figary
75 Nobody's Jig
76 Paul's Steeple
77 Paul's Wharf
78 The Queen's Jig (original tune)
79 Row Well, Ye Mariners
80 Under and Over/The Jovial Tinker/Jones' Ale

Processional Double Circle for as Many as Will (5)
81 Basilina (no tune yet found)
82 The Black Almain
83 The Earl of Essex Measure
84 Tinternell
85 Turkeloney

Single File for as Many as Will (1)
86 The Farandole (no tune given)

Tunes only (Dance directions lost) (11)
All Flowers of the Broom
Barley Break
The Cushion Dance
Downright Squire/The Upright Esquier
I Care Not for These Ladies
John, Come Kiss Me Now
Mall Sims
Packington's Pownde
Peggy Ramsey
Rural Dance about the Maypole
Watkin's Ale

Names only (Dance directions and tunes lost) (3)
The Jolly Joiner
Tom Tiler
The Vicar of Saint Fools

ALTHEA   (Moderate-Difficult)   32 Bars

Two-couple square set.

First Verse

A1 Partners take near hands and lead forward a double and fall back again to places; partners set to eachother as follows: land on the right foot and kick right with the left, then land on the left foot and kick left with the right, then jump in place three times, crossing the feet each time.

A2 Repeat A1.

B1 Partners move forward (without hands) and cross over by right shoulders and change places with opposites, then set as in A1.

B2 Repeat B1 back to places.

Second Verse

A1 Partners side to right shoulders and then set as in First Verse.

A2 Partners side to left shoulders and then set as in First Verse.

B1 1 Man casts off to his left and, followed by 1 Woman, returns to his place; all set to partners as in First Verse.

B2 The 2 couple does the cast-off figure of B1; all set as in First Verse.

Third Verse

A1 Partners arm right and set to eachother as in First Verse.

A2 Partners arm left and set to eachother as in First Verse.

B1 1 Man and 2 Woman move forward a double, meet and stand back to back, take hands and turn once around clockwise back to places while the 2 Man and 1 Woman skip around them counter-clockwise back to places.

B2 Repeat B1 with numbers changed.

The first half of the unusual setting step described in "Althea" has been revived as a popular step in New England contra-dancing, known as the Balance (as in "Petronella," for example). Sharp arrived at a different interpretation for the B section of the First Verse, necessitating a distortion of the music. Therefore, if the version of the tune on record EFDSS PLA-2 is used, the instructions for the B section of the First Verse alone should be repeated in order to fit the distorted music.

Playford III
Sharp III 49

CUCKOLDS ALL A-ROW   (Moderate-Difficult)   24 Bars

Two-couple square set.

First Verse

A1 Couples take near hands, move forward a double and meet their opposites and fall back a double to places.
A2 Repeat A1.
B1 1 Man and 2 Woman back-to-back while 2 Man and 1 Woman do the same. The same couples then do a gypsy (clockwise, facing).
B2 Partners back-to-back, followed by a gypsy (clockwise, facing).

Second Verse

A1 Partners side to right shoulders.
A2 Opposites side to left shoulders.
B1 The two Men change places; then the Women change places; all four circle clockwise once around.
B2 The two Women change places; then the Men change places; all four circle clockwise once around back to original places.

Third Verse

A1 Partners arm right.
A2 Opposites arm left.
B1 Opposites take both hands and do a clockwise half-poussette to change places. The Men cast off to their right and, followed by their partners, return in a small circle to the same places.
B2 Continue the broken poussette of B1 back to original places. The Men cast off to their left and, followed by their partners, return in a small circle to original places.

This tune was originally used for the satirical song about Mary Queen of Scots that is, in part, well known to children:
"Mistress Mary, quite contrary,
How does your garden grow?
With cockle shells and silver bells
And cuckolds all a-row."

Charles II admitted that this was one of his favorite dances in 1662, at which time it was described as "old." Chappell thought this tune was used for a Cavalier song "Hey boys, Up Go We," but it turns out he was mistaken, for there is a completely separate tune and dance to that name. Nevertheless, Sharp believed Chappell.

Playford I
Sharp II 99
Chappell 340

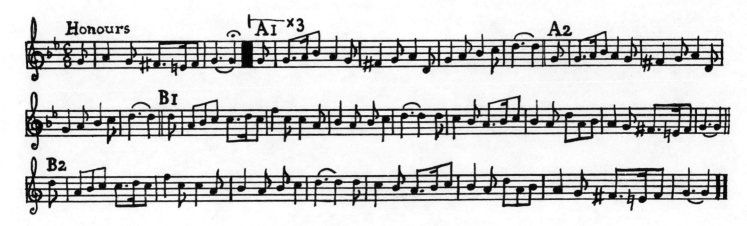

Two-couple square set.

First Verse

A1 Partners take near hands, move forward a double and fall back again.

A2 Repeat A1

Chorus

B1 All face partners; all fall back a double and come forward a double. Then opposites do a right-hand turn once around.

B2 All face opposites; all fall back a double and come forward again. Then partners do a left-hand turn once around.

Second Verse

A1 Partners side to right shoulders.

A2 Partners side to left shoulders.

B1 & 2 Chorus

Third Verse

A1 Partners arm right.

A2 Partners arm left.

B1 & 2 Chorus.

"Heartsease" is mentioned as a dance in the play "Misogonus" ca. 1560, and in Shakespeare's "Romeo & Juliet" in 1597.

"Sing care away and sport and play;
Pastime is all our pleasure;
If well we fare, for nought we care;
In mirth consists our treasure.
Let lankies lurk and drudges work,
We do defy their slavery;
He is but a fool that goes to school;
All we delight in bravery."

Playford I
Sharp IV 42
Chappell 210

Two-couple square set.

First Verse

A1   Couples take near hands, move forward a double, meet, and fall back a double again to places.
A2   Repeat A1.

Chorus

B1   Couples, right hand to right hand, move forward a double and meet. Opposites take left hand to left hand and lead out a double to each Man's left.
B2   Changing to right hand to right hand, lead back into the middle a double, meet, and take right hand to right hand with partner; fall back a double to places.
C1 & 2   Starting by facing partners, do four changes of a circular hey.

Second Verse

A1   Partners side to right shoulders.
A2   Partners side to left shoulders.
B & C   Chorus.

Third Verse

A1   Partners arm right.
A2   Partners arm left.
B & C   Chorus.

For some reason, Sharp set this dance to the tune of "Daphne" rather than the original tune, and this necessitated a faster hey at the end of each chorus. The original tune is used here.

Playford I
Sharp IV 43
Chappell 147

ROGERO   (Moderate)   32 Bars

Two-couple square set.

First Verse

A1   1s skip clockwise around the set and back to places.
A2   1s skip counterclockwise around the set and back to places.

Chorus—I

B1   1 Man and both Women meet and circle-three once around the 2 Man clockwise.
B2   1 Woman and both Men do likewise around the 2 Woman.

Second Half of First Verse

A1   2s skip clockwise around the set and back to places.
A2   2s skip counter-clockwise around the set and back to places.

Chorus—II

B1   2 Man and both Women meet and circle-three once around the 1 Man clockwise.
B4   2 Woman and both Men do likewise around the 1 Woman.

Second Verse

A1   Partners side to right shoulders.
A2   Partners side to left shoulders.
B1 & 2   Chorus I.
A3   Opposites side to right shoulders.
A4   Opposite side to left shoulders.
B3 & 4   Chorus II.

Third Verse

A1   Partners arm right.
A2   Partners arm left.
B1 & 2   Chorus I.
A3   Opposites arm right.
A4   Opposites arm left.
B3 & 4   Chorus II.

The tune is at least as old as 1557 and was danced at least as early as 1579. Melusine Wood noted an Italian dance "Ruggiero" but the notes are confusing enough to require a certain amount of interpretation, as given here. Wood herself suggests in an earlier work that Rogero could be the same as "Sir Roger de Coverley" (Playford, 1695), but that is hardly likely, and Ruggiero fits the tune well. The tune, found in William Ballet's Lute Book (Trinity College, Dublin, 1600), Dallis' Lute Book (Trinity College, Dublin) and the Dowland manuscripts at the Public Library, Cambridge, was used to set the words of many contemporary songs. The words given here were written by Deloney about 1598 for this tune:
"When as the Duke of Normandy with glist'ring spear and shield
Had entered into fair England and foil'd his foes in field."

Chappell 93

RUFTY TUFTY   (Easy)   28 Bars

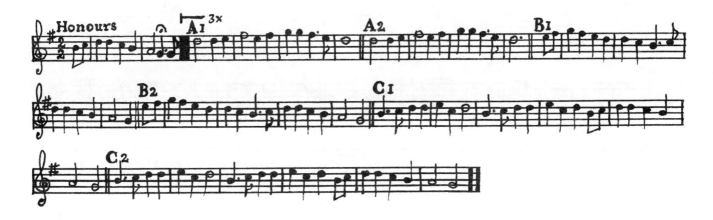

Two-couple square set.
First Verse

A1 Partners take near hands, move forward a double and meet and fall back a double again to places.
A2 Repeat A1.

Chorus

B1 Partners set to eachother and turn single.
B2 Repeat 1.
C1 1 Man with left hand to left hand leads partner out a double to his right (the "left" wall) and leads back in a double to places right hand to right hand, while the 2 Man and his partner do likewise (to the "right" wall and back); all turn single.
C2 1 Man with right hand to right hand leads 2 Woman out ("up") a double and leads back a double to places left hand to left hand, while the 2 Man and 1 Woman do likewise ("down"); all turn single.

Second Verse

A1 Partners side to right shoulders.
A2 Partners side to left shoulders.
B & C Chorus.

Third Verse

A1 Partners arm right.
A2 Partners arm left.
B & C Chorus.

Playford I
Sharp II 86

Holbein II

23

Three-couple circular set.
First Verse

A1   All take hands and slip eight slips clockwise.
A2   Slip eight slips counter-clockwise back to places.

Chorus

B1   The 1s take near hands and lead forward a double and fall back a double to places; then the 1s lead between the 2s and 3s, separate and cast back to places around the outside of the circle, using a skipping step after they separate.

B2   The 2s do a similar figure to B1, passing between the 3s and 1s.

B3   The 3s do a similar figure to B1, passing between the 1s and 2s.

Second Verse

A1   Partners side to right shoulders.
A2   Partners side to left shoulders.
B1-3   Chorus (best to start figure with 2s).

Third Verse

A1   Partners arm right.
A2   Partners arm left.
B1-3   Chorus (best to start figure with 3s).

Playford III
Sharp IV 36

GREENWOOD   (Difficult)   8 Bars

This dance has an unusual formation: it is a circle for three couples, but flattened into a longways shape for much of its course. It starts as a circle.

Chorus

A1 All take hands and move forward a double into the center and fall back a double again to places; partners set and turn single.

A2 Partners take near hands and lead out a double, change hands and lead back a double to places; partners set and turn single.

First Verse

A1 2 Man sides to right shoulders with 1 Woman while the other Men side with eachother and the other Women side with eachother, then all set and turn single.

A2 Corners side to left shoulders; set and turn single.

A3 Partners side to right shoulders, set and turn single.

A4 & 5 Chorus.

Second Verse

A1 Same people who sided in A1 of First verse arm right, set and turn single.

A2 Corners arm left; set and turn single.

A3 Partners arm right; set and turn single.

A4 & 5 Chorus.

Third Verse

A1 1s circle clockwise with 3 Man while 2s circle with 3 Woman; set and turn single.

A2 3s circle with the 2 Man while 1s circle with the 2 Woman; set and turn single.

A3 2s circle with 1 Man while 3s circle with 1 Woman; set and turn single.

A4 & 5 Chorus.

Fourth Verse

A1 Those who circled in A1 of Third Verse, partners starting by passing right shoulders do a straight hey; set and turn single.

A2 Those who circled in A2 of Third Verse do straight hey; set and turn single.

A3 Those who circled in A3 of Third Verse do straight hey; set and turn single.

A4 & 5 Chorus.

Fifth Verse

A1 Men take hands and circle once around clockwise; partners set and turn single.

A2 Women circle once around; partners set and turn single.

A3 & 4 Chorus.

Sixth Verse

A1 Starting by passing partners by the right, Men do a weaving figure once around the set; partners set and turn single.

A2 Women do a similar figure, starting by passing partners by left shoulders; partners set and turn single.

A3 & 4 Chorus.

The tune was known in Henry VIII's reign.
"Shall I go walk the woods so wild wandring wandring here and there; As I was once full sore beguiled; alas for love I die of woe."

Playford I
Sharp IV 55
Chappell 66

JENNY PLUCK PEARS   (Easy-Moderate)   **24 Bars**

Three-couple circular set.
First Verse

A1   All take hands and slip around the circle eight slips clockwise; partners set and turn single.
A2   All slip back counterclockwise to places; partners set and turn single.

Chorus

B1   1 Man takes partner, right hand to right hand, and puts her in the middle, facing him; then 2 Man does like-
wise with his partner; then 3 Man does likewise with his partner; partners honour eachother.
A3   While Women are thus standing in the center back to back, Men skip around them clockwise.
A4   Men skip counter-clockwise around back to places.
B2   1 Man takes partner, left hand to left hand, and brings her back to her place; then the 2 Man does likewise
with his partner; then the 3 Man does likewise with his partner; partners honour eachother.

Second Verse

A1   Partners side to right shoulders; set and turn single.
A2   Partners side to left shoulders; set and turn single.
B1-B2   Chorus (but this time the Women put the Men into the center, left hand to left hand, and take them out
right hand to right hand).

Third Verse

A1   Partners arm right; set and turn single.
A2   Partners arm left; set and turn single.
B1-B2   Chorus (same as chorus of First Verse).

Playford I
Sharp II 63

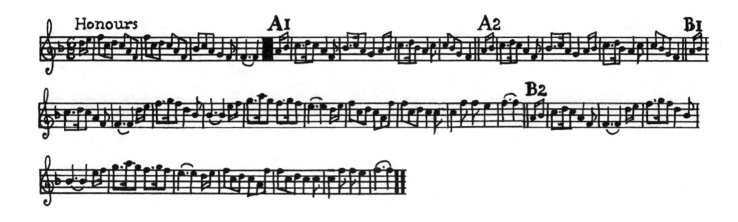

Three-couple circular set.

First Verse

A1   All take hands and come forward a double into the center and fall back a double again to places.

A2   Repeat A1

B1   1 Man and 3 Woman come forward and take right hands; then 2 Man and 1 Woman do the same; then 3 Man and 2 Woman do the same; then all move the six-hand star thus formed once around to places.

B2   1 Man and 3 Woman honour; then 2 Man and 1 Woman honour; then 3 Man and 2 Woman honour; then all do a six-handed left-hand star once around to places. Note: in this dance, "honour" replaces "kiss" in the original.

Second Verse

A1   Partners side to right shoulders.

A2   Partners side to left shoulders.

B1   Repeat B1 figure from First Verse.

B2   1 Man and 2 Woman honour; then 2 Man and 3 Woman honour; then 3 Man and 1 Woman honour; then all do a six-handed left-hand star once around to places.

Third Verse

A1   Partners arm right.

A2   Partners arm left.

B1   Repeat B1 figure from First Verse.

B2   1 Man and 1 Woman honour; then 2 Man and 2 Woman honour, then 3 Man and 3 Woman honour; then all do a six-handed left-hand star once around to places.

Slight alterations have been made to Sharp's interpretation of this dance. Sharp also did not supply the original tune and had to add figures to compensate for the ill fit of the new tune, but the original tune is used here. Dancers will recognise the original tune as an earlier version of the popular longways dance "Valentine's Day"; no doubt Sharp discarded it because Playford's printer had badly garbled it, so that he failed to recognise what it was meant to be.

Playford IV
Sharp VI 66

Three-couple circular set.
First Verse
A1 All take hands and slip around the circle eight slips clockwise; partners set and turn single.
A2 All slip counter-clockwise eight slips back to places; partners set and turn single.

Chorus
A3 1 Man leads 1 and 2 Women forward a double towards the 3 Woman and then they fall back a double. 1 Man turns the 3 Woman with two hands while the 1 and 2 Women turn eachother. 1 Man ends the figure standing to the left of the Woman he has just turned.
A4 As in A3, 1 Man leads 3 and 1 Women towards 2 Woman, etc.
A5 As in A3, 1 Man leads 2 and 3 Women towards 1 Woman, etc.

Second Verse
A1 Partners side to right shoulders; set and turn single.
A2 Partners side to left shoulders, set and turn single.
A3-5 Chorus (with 2 Man doing as 1 Man did).

Third Verse
A1 Partners arm right, set and turn single.
A2 Partners arm left, set and turn single.
A3-5 Chorus (with 3 Man doing as 1 Man did).

This was mentioned as a country dance in Heywood's *A Woman Kill'd with Kindness*, Act I, scene 2, and in Fletcher's *Love's Cure*, Act II, scene 2.

Playford IV
Sharp IV 34
Chappell 193

PUTNEY FERRY   (Moderate)   40 Bars

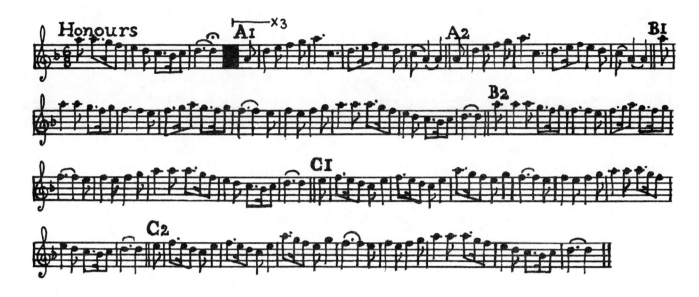

Three-couple circular set.
First Verse

A1   All take hands and slip eight slips clockwise.
A2   All slip counter-clockwise back to places.

Chorus

B1   Men form an outward-facing circle in the middle, take hands and dance around clockwise back to places, while Women turn single clockwise and again counter-clockwise.
B2   Women do what Men did in B1 and vice versa.
C1   Each Man sets to his corner, then to his opposite; then partners honour and do a two-hand turn.
C2   Each Woman sets to her corner, then to her opposite; then partners honour and do a two-hand turn.

Second Verse

A1   Partners side to right shoulders
A2   Partners side to left shoulders.
B & C   Chorus.

Third Verse

A1   Partners arm right.
A2   Partners arm left.
B & C   Chorus.

Putney Ferry was at a village on the Thames River just upstream from Elizabethan London. Putney Bridge stands today on the site of the ferry, and Putney itself was long ago absorbed into London. The dance was mentioned in *Misogonus*, ca. 1560.

Playford IV
Sharp II 66

Three-couple longways set.

First Verse

A1   Partners take near hands and lead up a double and fall back again; partners set and turn single.
A2   Repeat A1.

Chorus

B1   1 couple shake right hands, then the 2 couple likewise, then the 3 couple likewise; then partners shake left hands, then kiss twice and do a two-hand turn (note: if it is not desirable to kiss partners, some other movement, such as clapping hands, may be substituted).
B2   Each Man shakes right hands with his partner, then with his corner, then with his partner again, then shake left hands with his partner. Then each Man kiss his partner twice and partners do a two-hand turn.

Second Verse

A1   Partners side to right shoulders, set and turn single.
A2   Partners side to left shoulders, set and turn single.
B1 & 2   Chorus.

Third Verse

A1   Partners arm right, set and turn single.
A2   Partners arm left, set and turn single.
B1 & 2   Chorus.

"All in a garden green two lovers sat at ease
As they could scarce be seen among, among the leafy trees.
They long had loved y-fere, and no longer than truly,
In that time of the year cometh 'twixt May and July."

The song was published by William Pickering in 1565 and many subsequent times in the sixteenth century. The tune is in William Ballet's Lute Book.

Playford I
Chappell 110

Three-couple longways set.

First Verse

A1   Partners take near hands and lead up a double and fall back again.

A2   Repeat A1.

B1   1 and 3 Men face Men's wall while 1 and 3 Women face Women's wall; All move forward a double and fall back a double. With the 2s falling back slightly, each line makes a separate circle with hands and moves around half way to invert the set (Sharp says once around, but half-way seems more logical).

B2   Repeat B1 back to places.

Second Verse

A1   Partners side to right shoulders.

A2   Partners side to left shoulders.

B1   1s face down while 3s face up; 1s and 3s change places, the 1s passing between the 3s, while the 2s fall back a double and come forward a double again.

B2   3s face down while 1s face up; 1s and 3s change places, the 3s passing between the 1s, while the 2s to the same as in B1.

Third Verse

A1   Partners arm right.

A2   Partners arm left.

B1   All take hands along the lines and fall back a double and come forward again; each line does half a straight hey, starting with the 1s and 2s passing by right shoulders.

B2   All take hands along the lines and fall back a double and come forward again; each line completes the hey back to places.

Chappell can find no mention of this tune in print before the reign of James I, but both tune and dance would appear to be sixteenth-century.

Playford I
Sharp II 104
Chappell 271

THE BLACK NAG (Moderate) 24 Bars

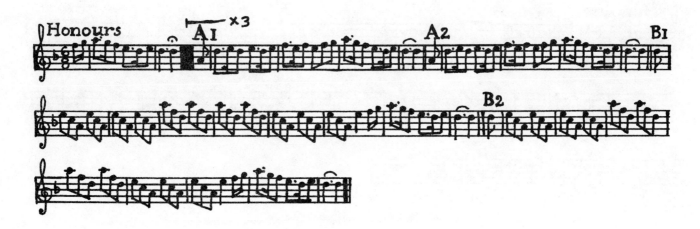

Three-couple longways set.

First Verse

A1 Partners join near hands and lead up a double and fall back again.
A2 Repeat A1.
B1 1s take both hands and slip four slips up; then the 2s do likewise; then the 3s do likewise; all turn single.
B2 3s take two hands and slip four slips down; then 2s do likewise; then 1s do likewise; all turn single.

Second Verse

A1 Partners side to right shoulders.
A2 Partners side to left shoulders.
B1 1 Man and 3 Woman aim their right shoulders at eachother and, using a slipping step, change places, passing back to back; then 3 Man and 1 Woman do likewise; then 2s do likewise; all turn single.
B2 Repeat B1 back to places.

Third Verse

A1 Partners arm right.
A2 Partners arm left.
B1 1 Man facing down while 2 and 3 Men face up, the Men do a straight hey for three, the 1 and 2 Men starting by passing by right shoulders, using a skipping step.
B2 Women do what Men did in B1. Note: it is traditional, although not in Playford's instructions, for the Men to turn single in the last two bars of the Women's hey.

Playford IV
Sharp II 108

Three-couple longways set.
First Verse

A1   Partners take near hands, lead up a double and fall back again; partners set and turn single.

A2   Repeat A1.

B1   2 Man does a hey for three with the 1s (starting by passing 1 Woman by right shoulders) while the 2 Woman heys with the 3s (starting by passing 3 Man by right shoulders); then partners turn once around clockwise with two hands.

B2   2 Man heys with the 3s (starting by passing left shoulders with the 3 Woman) while the 2 Woman heys with the 1s (starting by passing the 1 Man by left shoulders. Partners turn with two hands.

Second Verse

A1   Partners side to right shoulders, set and turn single.

A2   Partners side to left shoulders, set and turn single.

B1   2 Man circles half-way around with the 1s and open out into a straight line facing down with the 2 Man in the middle, while 2 Woman does likewise with the 3s, ending by facing up. Still holding near hands, all fall back a single and come forward a single. Partners do a two-hand turn, the 2s once and a quarter around while the others turn just once around; all are now improper.

B2   Repeat B1 back to places, the 2 Man circling with the 3s and the 2 Women with the 1s.

Third Verse

A1   Partners arm right, set and turn single.

A2   Partners arm left, set and turn single.

B1   1 Man, 2 Woman and 3 Man take hands and circle once around clockwise (best with the 2 Man in the middle of the ring); the 2s then do a two-hand turn once around.

B2   1 Woman, 2 Man and 3 Woman take hands and circle once around clockwise (best with the 2 Woman in the middle of the ring); the 2s then do a two-hand turn once around.

This is a bagpipe tune (bagpipes were not then or now limited to Scotland and the Scottish form), of which a variant was used as an Elizabethan Morris tune "Trip and Go."

"Trip & go, heave & ho, up & down, to & fro,
From the town to the grove, two & two let us rove,
A-maying, a-playing, love hath no gainsaying,
So trip & go, trip & go, merrily trip & go."

Playford I
Sharp IV 44
Chappell 270

CHESTNUT/DOVE'S FIGARY (Moderate) 24 Bars

Three-couple longways set.

First Verse

A1 Partners take near hands, lead up a double and fall back again.

A2 Repeat A1.

B1 All take hands along the lines, fall back a single, then come forward, passing partners by right shoulders, and cross over to the opposite sides. Then, with the 2s falling back slightly, each line makes a separate circle, and dances half-way around clockwise to open out into a straight line with inverted set.

B2 Repeat B1 back to places.

Second Verse

A1 Partners side to right shoulders.

A2 Partners side to left shoulders.

B1 All take hands along the lines, fall back a single, then come forward, passing partners by right shoulders, and cross over to the opposite sides. Then each line does half a straight hey (1s facing down, 2s and 3s facing up, 1s and 2s starting by passing by right shoulders) to invert the set.

B2 Repeat B1 back to places, but beginning the heys at the bottom.

Third Verse

A1 Partners arm right.

A2 Partners arm left.

B1 All take hands along the lines, fall back a single, then come forward, passing partners by right shoulders, and cross over to the opposite sides. Then the 1s, taking near hands, lead down the middle to bottom place, followed by the 2s and 3s to invert the set.

B2 Repeat B1 back to places, but with 1s casting up the outside followed by the others.

Playford I
Sharp II 106

34

Three-couple longways set
First Verse

A1   Partners take near hands and lead up a double and fall back a double to places.

A2   Repeat A1

B1   1s cross over by right shoulders, go down the outside of the set one place while 2s move up; 1s cross over again through second place by the right shoulders and go down the outside of the set one place while the 3s move up.

B2   New top couple repeats B1

B3   New top couple repeats B1

Second Verse

A1   Partners side to right shoulders

A2   Partners side to left shoulders

B1   1s face down while others face up, and do half a straight hey starting by passing right shoulders; partners face and set.

B2   All turn single. Then 1s face up and others face down, and do half a straight hey, starting by passing left shoulders.

B3   Partners face, set and turn single.

Third Verse

A1   Partners arm right

A2   Partners arm left

B1   The 2s falling back, each line forms a circle and moves half way around (Men clockwise and Woman counter-clockwise) to invert the set; partners face and set.

B2   All turn single; then, the 2s falling back, each line forms a circle and moves half way around (Men counter-clockwise and Women clockwise).

B3   Partners face, set and turn single.

As is so often the case, Playford's text has omitted a few words; Sharp attempted to remedy the deficiency, but his interpretation is at variance with this one.

Playford I
Sharp VI 68

GREENSLEEVES (and Yellow Lace)   (Difficult)   32 Bars

Three-couple longways set.

First Verse

A1 1s set and cast off into second place, the 2s moving up; then the 2s set and cast off into second place, the 1s moving up.

A2 Repeat A1.

B1 1 Man goes down the middle to dance a figure-8 around the 3s, starting by passing the 3 Woman by left shoulders, while the 1 Woman (following after him) dances a figure-8 around the 2s, starting by passing the 2 Man by right shoulders.

B2 1s pass eachother by right shoulders; the 1 Man dances a figure-8 around the 2s, starting by passing the 2 Woman by right shoulders, while the 1 Woman dances a figure-8 around the 3s, starting by passing the 3 Man by right shoulders.

Second Verse

A1 The 1s pass eachother by right shoulders. 1 Man joins hands with the 2s and they circle one and a half times around clockwise to open up into a line across the set facing down, the 1 Man in the middle of the line; while the 1 Woman circles similarly with the 3s, whose line ends facing up; the 2s and 3s are improper. The 1s then pass eachother by right shoulders and the 1 Man joins hands with the 3s while the 1 Woman joins hands with the 2s.

A2 Each group circles once and a half around clockwise and opens out to form lines across the set, the top line facing down and the bottom line facing up; the 1s are in the middle and the 2s and 3s are proper once again. Then the 1s pass eachother by right shoulders again.

B1 1 Man dances a straight hey for three with the 3s, starting by passing the 3 Woman by left shoulders, while the 1 Woman dances a hey with the 2s, starting by passing the 2 Man by left shoulders. The 1s pass eachother by right shoulders again.

B2 1 Man dances a straight hey for three with the twos, starting by passing the 2 Woman by right shoulders, while the 1 Woman dances a hey with the 3s, starting by passing the 3 Man by right shoulders. 1s meet in the middle and cast to the foot, the 2s and 3s moving up, and the dance begins again with new number 1 couple.

The tune is Elizabethan, but the dance was not published until 1721 when it took the form of a triple-minor longways, although it is better suited as a three-couple dance. Elizabethan dancers used all the figures found here, so it is not impossible that the dance is much earlier than 1721. "Greensleeves" was recorded as a dance by 1593.

Playford, vol. I, 1721
Chappell 116, 227-233.
Country Dance Book,
New Series

Three-couple longways set.

First Verse

A1   Partners take near hands, lead up a double and fall back again; partners set and turn single.

A2   Repeat A1.

B1 & 2   1s face down while 2s and 3s face up, and all do a mirror hey. A skipping step may be used.

Second Verse

A1   Partners side to right shoulders, set and turn single.

A2   Partners side to left shoulders, set and turn single.

B1 & 2   Repeat the mirror heys of the first verse, but with those who are "bulging" in middle positions raising their hands to form an arch, while the others go under the various arches thus formed.

Third Verse

A1   Partners arm right, set and turn single.

A2   Partners arm left, set and turn single.

B1   While the 2s and 3s face up, the 1s cross over by left shoulders and begin a straight hey on the improper sides by passing the 2s by right shoulders (note: these are not mirror heys).

B2   While the 2s and 3s remain on their own sides, the 1s cross back over to their own sides, passing by right shoulders, when they reach the foot in B1; the hey is then continued until all are back in original places. Note: the 2s and 3s may have to exaggerate the loops of their heys so as not to have to pause to wait for the 1s to cross over at the foot.

A version of this tune was arranged and published by the German composer Michael Praetorius in his book *Terpsichore* (1612); he calls it "Tanz der Bauerinnen" or Farm Girls' Dance.

Playford I
Sharp II 102

MAIDEN LANE   (Moderate-Difficult)   **24 Bars**

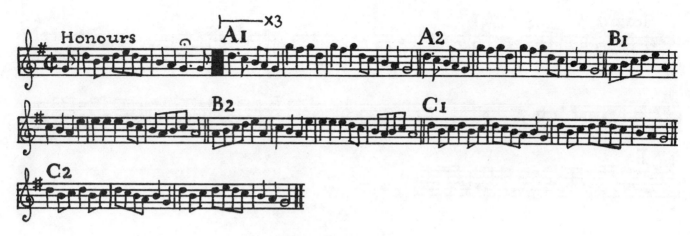

Three-couple longways set.
First Verse
A1   Partners take near hands and lead up a double and fall back again.
A2   Repeat A1.
B1   Still facing up, all slip four slips to the left and four slips back again to places.
B2   Each line does a straight hey, the 1s facing down and the others facing up, starting by passing right shoulders.
C1   Partners face, set and turn single
C2   Repeat C1. Note: the set remains inverted.

Second Verse
A1   Partners side to right shoulders
A2   Partners side to left shoulders
B1   All fall back a single, then partners cross over by right shoulders and change places.
B2   Repeat B1 back to places.
C1   Partners set and turn single
C2   Repeat C1. Note: the set still remains inverted.

Third Verse
A1   Partners arm right
A2   Partners arm left
B1   1 Man and 2 Woman change places by right shoulders; then 2 Man changes places with 1 Woman while 3 Man changes places with 3 Woman.
B2   1 Man changes places with 3 Woman; then 3 Man changes places with 1 Woman, both the 3s immediately moving down to last place on the outside while 2 Man changes places with 2 Woman as they move up the middle.
C1   All set and turn single
C2   Repeat C1.

Playford I
Sharp III 64

Three-couple longways set.

First Verse

A1   Partners take near hands and lead up a double and fall back again. Do that again.

A2   1 Man change places (by right shoulders) with 2 Woman and then continue moving to change places with the 3 Man; then all lead up a double and fall back again.

A3   1 Woman change places with 2 Man and then with 3 Woman; all lead up a double and fall back again.

A4-7   Whoever is in 1 Man's place and whoever is in 1 Woman's place alternate the place-changing figures of A2 and A3 until all are back in original places.

Second Verse

A1   Partners side to right shoulders, then side to left shoulders.

A2   1s and 2s do "shuttle" figure: 1s take both hands and slip down the middle while 2s "bulge" and slip up the outside and then the 2s slip down the middle while the 1s slip up the outside; 1s and 2s repeat the figure. Meanwhile, the 3s, using a skipping step, cross over by right shoulders and go completely around the outside of the set and return to bottom places.

A3   2s and 3s do "shuttle" figure, starting with the 3s slipping up the middle while the 2s slip down the outside; meanwhile, the 1s skip completely around the set and return to places.

Third Verse

A1   Partners arm right, then arm left.

A2-4   The Men, using a skipping step, dance a "sheepskin" hey around the Women, who stand still: 1 Man, followed by the 2 and 3 Men, crosses over and starts a weaving figure through the Women, starting by passing the 1 Woman by right shoulders; when the last Man has passed the 2 Woman, he doubles back around her just before the 1 Man passes her on his way back, so the formerly trailing Man is now leading, but not for long, as the new trailing Man turns back around the 2 Woman in order to take the lead, and finally the original 1 Man turns back around the 2 Woman to take the lead back again. Then the 1 Man, followed by the 2 and 3 Men, casts off down the outside of the Women's line, leads across the foot and up the Men's side back to places.

A5-7   The Women dance a mirror-image of that same sheepskin hey around the Men.

The original tune is given here, but Sharp thought it dull so he substituted the tune of "Lavena," given here as second tune.

Playford I
Sharp IV 50

39

SCOTCH CAP   (Moderate-Difficult)   24 Bars

Three-couple longways set.

First Verse

A1 Partners take near hands and lead up a double and fall back again.
A2 Repeat A1.
B1 The 2 and 3 Men and the 1 and 2 Women fall back a single and then, passing by right shoulders, cross over di-agonally and change places, the 2 Man with the 1 Woman and the 3 Man with the 2 Woman; then the 1 Man and 3 Woman cross over by right shoulders and change places.
B2 Repeat B1 back to places.

Second Verse

A1 Partners side to right shoulders.
A2 Partners side to left shoulders.
B1 Take hands along the lines, fall back a double and come forward again. Then the 1 Man arms right with the 3 Man while the 1 Woman arms right with the 3 Woman and the 2s arm right.
B2 Take hands along the lines, fall back a double and come forward again. Partners do a two-hand turn once around.

Third Verse

A1 Partners arm right.
A2 Partners arm left.
B1 Take hands along the lines; the Men slip four slips up to their left while the Women slip four slips down to their left. Then, before the mid-point of the musical phrase, the two lines begin a hey with hands back to places, the 3 Man beginning by giving right hand to the 1 Woman.
B2 The Men slip down to their right while the Women slip up to their right; as before, dance a hey back to places, the 1 Man beginning by giving left hand to the 3 Woman.

Playford I
Sharp IV 53

Three-couple longways set.
First Verse
A1   Taking near hands, partners lead up a double and fall back again.

A2   Repeat A1.

B1   The 2s "bulge" and slip up to top place while the 1s go to the foot, passing outside the 3s who belatedly move into second places, going up the middle.

B2   Repeat B1 with new numbers.

B3   Repeat B1 with new numbers back to original places.

Second Verse
A1   Partners side to right shoulders.

A2   Partners side to left shoulders.

B1   The 1s cross over by right shoulders, cast down and cross again below the 2s and cast again into last place, the 2s and 3s all the while moving up when appropriate.

B2   Repeat B1 with new numbers.

B3   Repeat B1 with new numbers back to original places.

Third Verse
A1   Partners arm right.

A2   Partners arm left.

B1   First corners cross by right shoulders, then second corners cross while the 3s change places.

B2   1 Man (in second place improper) change places with 3 Woman, then 1 Woman change places with 3 Man while the 2s change places.

B3   Partners set and turn single.

Note: since the last verse is progressive, the whole dance may be repeated twice more to give each couple a chance to be number one.

"Can you dance the shaking of the sheets,
A dance that everyone must do?
Can you trim it up with dainty sweets
And everything that b'longs thereto?
Make ready then your winding-sheet
And see how ye can bestir your feet,
For Death is the man that all must meet,
For Death is the man that all must meet."

This dance was mentioned as a dance in the play *Misogonus*, ca. 1560, and in many subsequent publications. A different tune with the same title is in William Ballet's Lute Book, but the tune fits neither the dance nor the words of the song.

Playford I
Sharp VI 70
Chappell 84

Three-couple longways set

First Verse

A1 Partners take near hands and lead up a double and fall back again. Partners change places by right shoulders.

A2 Partners take near hands and lead down a double and fall back. Partners change places back again.

B1 The 1s slip down to stand inside the 2s; then the 3s slip up to stand outside the 2s. The 1 Man, followed by the other men, casts off in a circle to his left to bring all back to places, while the Women do likewise to the right.

B2 The 3s slip up and stand in front of the 2s; then the 1s slip down and stand behind the 2s. The 3 Man, followed by the other Men, casts off to the right in a circle to bring all back to places, while the Women do likewise to the left.

Second Verse

A1 Partners side to right shoulders and then change places.

A2 Partners side to left shoulders and then change places back.

B1 Taking hands along the lines, all fall back a double and come forward a double. Then, with the 2s falling back slightly, the Men circle once around clockwise, while the Women do the same, back to places.

B2 Taking hands along the lines, all fall back a double and come forward a double. With the 2s falling back slightly, all turn about and form outward-facing circles and move the circles once around back to places.

Third Verse

A1 Partners arm right and then change places.

A2 Partners arm left and then change places back again.

B1 1 Man changes places with 2 Woman; then 2 Man changes places with 1 Woman; then the 3s cross over and skip up the outside of the set to first places improper, the other couples moving down one place.

B2 3 Woman changes places with 2 Man; then 2 Woman changes places with the 3 Man; then the 1s cross over and skip up the outside of the set to first places, the other couples moving down.

Playford I
Sharp III 69

Three-couple longways set.

First Verse

A1   Partners take near hands, lead up a double and fall back again; partners set and turn single.
A2   Repeat A1.

Chorus

B1   Take hands along the lines, come forward a double and fall back again. Then the two lower Men raise their hands to make an arch and the two lower Women do the same, while the Top couple casts off down the outside and comes in through the arches and down to bottom places, the other couples moving up on the last two bars.*

B2   Repeat B1 with new top couple.
B3   Repeat B1 with new top couple, back to original places.

Second Verse

A1   Partners side to right shoulders, set and turn single.
A2   Partners side to left shoulders, set and turn single.
B1-3   Chorus.

Third Verse

A1   Partners arm right, set and turn single.
A2   Partners arm left, set and turn single.
B1-3   Chorus.

* Pat Shaw has turned this chorus inside-out by having the top couple lead down the middle and out through the arches rather than cast and lead in through the arches; most dancers use the Shaw pattern today, and there is certainly nothing wrong with it.

According to Chappell, the earliest surviving set of words to this tune dates from the early 1620s, but is not "desirable to reprint." Chappell supplies an alternative set of words published in 1707, but which could be much earlier:

"Upon a time I chance to walk along a green
Where pretty lasses danced in strife to choose a queen.
Some homely-dressed, some handsome, some pretty and some gay,
But who excelled in dancing must be queen of May.
Good fellows, great and small, pray let me you advise
To have a care withall; 'tis good to be merry and wise."

Playford I
Sharp III 71
Chappell 254

THE WHISH   (Difficult)   42 Bars

Three-couple longways set

First Verse

A1 Partners take near hands and lead up a double and fall back again. Partners face and set slightly forwards towards eachother, then fall back a single.

A2 Repeat A1.

A3 The 2 Man and 1 Man lead out between their partners, separate and cast back to places, then arm left.

A4 The 2 Man and 3 Man lead out between their partners, separate and cast back to places, then arm right.

A5 The 2 and 1 Women repeat A3, arming right.

A6 The 2 and 3 Women repeat A4, arming left.

Second Verse

A1 Partners side to right shoulders, set forwards and fall back a single.

A2 Partners side to left shoulders, set forwards and fall back a single.

A3 The 2s lead up through the 1s, separate and cast back to places, then do a right-hand turn.

A4 The 2s lead down through the 3s, separate and cast back to places, then do a left-hand turn.

A5 The 2s lead out between the 1 and 3 Women, separate and cast back to places, then arm left.

A6 The 2s lead out between the 1 and 3 Men, separate and cast back to places, then arm right.

Third Verse

A1 Partners arm right, set forwards and fall back a single.

A2 Partners arm left, set forwards and fall back a single.

A3 The 2s do a full figure-8 up around the 1s.

A4 The 2s do a full figure-8 down around the 3s.

A5 The 2s lead out between the 1 and 3 Women, separate and cast back to places, then arm left.

A6 The 2s lead out between the 1 and 3 Men, separate and cast back to places, then arm right.

Playford I
Sharp VI 77

WOODY COCK   (Difficult)   16 Bars

Three-couple longways set.

First Verse

A1   Partners take near hands and lead up a double and fall back again.
A2   Repeat A1.
B1 & 2   Partners set and turn single, twice.

Second Verse

A1   The 2s take near hands and lead up between the 1s, separate, cast off and return to places.
A2   The 2s take (other) near hands and lead down between the 3s, separate and cast back to places.
B1 & 2   Partners set and turn single, twice.

Third Verse

A1   Partners side to right shoulders.
A2   Partners side to left shoulders.
B1 & 2   Partners set and turn single, twice.

Fourth Verse

A1   The 2s pass by left shoulders, the 2 Man dancing counter-clockwise around the 1 Woman while the 2 Woman dances counter-clockwise around the 3 Man, with a skipping step, and return to places.
A2   The 2s pass by right shoulders, the 2 Man dancing clockwise around the 3 Woman while the 2 Woman dances clockwise around the 1 Man, and return to places.
B1 & 2   Partners set and turn single, twice.

Fifth Verse

A1   Partners arm right.
A2   Partners arm left.
B1 & 2   Partners set and turn single, twice.

Sixth Verse

A1 & 2   Men, with a skipping step, do a straight hey for three.
B1 & 2   Partners set and turn single, twice.

Seventh Verse

A1 & 2   Women dance a straight hey for three.
B1 & 2   Partners set and turn single, twice.

Eighth Verse

A1 & 2   1s face eachother while 2s and 3s face up; all dance a progressive hey around the set and back to places.
B1 & 2   Partners set and turn single, twice.

The tune was published in a collection assembled by Giles Farnaby at the end of the sixteenth century.

Playford I

45

Four-couple longways set.

First Verse

A1   Partners take near hands and lead up a double and fall back again. Then 1s, followed by 2s, cast off and follow short circular paths back to places while 3s, followed by 4s, do likewise.

A2   Partners take near hands and lead down a double and fall back again. Then 2s, followed by 1s, cast off and come back to places while 4s, followed by 3s, do likewise.

A3   2s face eachother and fall back while 1s and 3s move towards eachother, meet, and circle once around clockwise and return to places.

A4   3s face eachother and fall back while 2s and 4s meet and circle.

Second Verse

A1   Partners side to right shoulders, set and turn single.

A2   Partners side to left shoulders, set and turn single.

A3   1 and 2 Men take both hands and change places while 1 and 2 Women do the same; then the bottom two couples do likewise; Partners set and turn single.

A4   Repeat A3 back to places.

Third Verse

A1   Partners arm right, set and turn single.

A2   Partners arm left, set and turn single.

A3   Taking near hands, 1s face up while 4s face down and 2 and 3 Men face the Men's wall and 2 and 3 Women face the Women's wall; All lead forward a double, change hands and lead back a double. All eight take hands and circle half-way around clockwise.

A4   Repeat A3 back to places.

This was mentioned in 1548 and may even be earlier, as in 1575 it was thought to be "ancient." The earliest words are garbled and lost. The words given here, possibly by Robert Crawford, were published in 1724 about the Scottish border area of Cowdenknowes, near Berwick; of the many recordings of this song, one of the nicest is by Archie Fisher on Topic 12TS 277. The song is of course much slower than the dance.

"How blithe was I each morn to see
My swain come o'er the hill.
He skipped the burn and flew to me;
I met him with good will.
O, the broom, the bonny, bonny, broom,
The broom of the Cowdenknowes!
Fain would I be in the North Country,
Tending my father's ewes."

Playford I
Sharp III 73
Chappell 233, 458, 613, 783

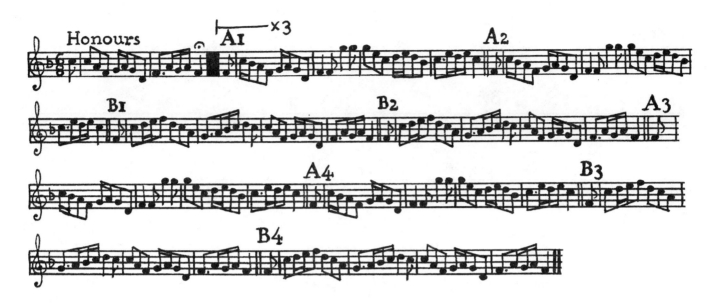

Four-couple longways set.

First Verse

A1   Partners take near hands and lead up a double and fall back again.
A2   Repeat A1.
B1   Partners set and turn single.
B2   Repeat B1.
A3 & 4   2 Man change places with 3 Woman; then 3 Man change places with 2 Woman. Then the top two couples form a ring while the bottom 2 couples do the same, and all thus circle once around clockwise.
B3 & 4   Repeat A3 & 4 back to places with changed numbers.

Second Verse

A1   Partners side to right shoulders.
A2   Partners side to left shoulders.
B1   Partners set and turn single.
B2   Repeat B1.
A3 & 4   All facing partners, 1s and 4s come forward a double while the 2s and 3s fall back a double. Then the 1s and 4s face down and up the set respectively and come forward a double and meet while the 2s and 3s slip four short slips up and down the set respectively. Then the 1 and 4 couples circle once around clockwise while the 2s and 3s turn partners with two hands once around.
B3 & 4   Repeat A3 & 4 back to places with changed numbers.

Third Verse

A1   Partners arm right.
A2   Partners arm left.
B1   Partners set and turn single.
B2   Repeat B1.
A3 & 4   With the middle two falling back slightly the Men circle once around clockwise; then the Women do likewise.
B3 & 4   With the 1s and 3s facing down and the 2s and 4s facing up, all do a straight hey for four on their own side.

Chappel reports that this tune, also sometimes known as "Mr. Webb's Fancy," was used to set parody songs during the English Civil War, but he was unable to find the original sixteenth-century words.

Playford I
Sharp II 110
Chappell 285

DAPHNE (Moderate) 28 Bars

Four-couple longways set.

First Verse

A1   Partners take near hands, lead up a double and fall back again.
A2   Repeat A1.

Chorus

B1   1s take both hands and slip down the middle of the set and back up again to places.
B2   4s do likewise, slipping up the set and back down again.
C1   1s, with a skipping step, cross over by right shoulders, cast down and cross over again below the 2s, cast and cross again below the 3s and cast down below bottom place, improper.
C2   1s continue criss-cross figure back up the set to original places. Note: an optional way of making the dance more interesting would be for the 1s to hurry through the criss-cross figure so as to leave enough time to cast to the foot at the end of it, the other couples moving up one place and changing their numbers accordingly; this will give other couples a chance to dance one round of the dance as 1s, especially if the First Verse is repeated after the Third Verse.

Second Verse

A1   Partners side to right shoulders.
A2   Partners side to left shoulders.
B-C   Chorus.

Third Verse

A1   Partners arm right.
A2   Partners arm left.
B-C   Chorus.

Chappell was unable to find "Daphne" in print any earlier than a 1626 example printed in the Netherlands, but it is probably at least 50 years older than that.

"When Daphne from fair Phoebus did fly
The west wind most sweetly did blow in her face.
Her silken scarf scarce shadowed her eyes;
The god cried 'O pity!' and held her in chase.
'Stay, nymph, stay, nymph,' cries Apollo,
'Tarry and turn thee, stay, nymph, stay;
Nor lion nor tiger doth thee follow;
Turn thy fair eyes and look this way.
O turn, pretty sweet, and let our lips meet,
O pity me, Daphne, pity me, O pity me, Daphne, pity me.' "

Playford I
Chappell 338
Van Cleef 4

48

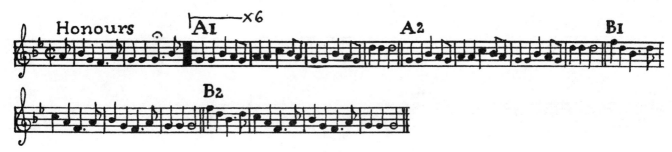

Four-couple longways set

First Verse

A1   Partners take near hands and lead up a double and fall back.

A2   Repeat A1

Chorus

B1   1s cast off, followed by the rest of their lines, and using a skipping step invert the set.

B2   1s cast back up to places, followed by the rest of their lines.

Second Verse

A1   Using a skipping step, the 1 Man leads his line across the top of the set and down behind the Women's line, while the 1 Woman leads her line inside the Men across the top of the set and to the bottom of where the Men's line was; the sets are now inverted and improper. The lines may take hands for this figure.

A2   Repeat A1 back to places, the 4 Man and 4 Woman leading.

B1 & 2   Chorus

Third Verse

A1   With the 2s and 3s falling back, each line forms a separate circle and slips around, the Men clockwise and the Women counter-clockwise.

A2   The circles reverse directions back to places.

B1 & 2   Chorus

Fourth Verse

A1   The two lines join together to form a large circle and slip left.

A2   Slip right back to places.

B1 & 2   Chorus

Fifth Verse

A1 & 2   1s and 3s face down while 2s and 4s face up. All do a straight hey for four in the separate lines, starting with passing right shoulders.

B1 & 2   Chorus

Sixth Verse

A1 & 2   All face as in the Fifth Verse, but do a circular hey once around the entire set.

B1 & 2   Chorus

This tune appears in the Fitzwilliam Virginal Book (which usually means it is from the 16th century), and has been used to set words of a great many ballads. The original words have been lost, but one early set reads:

"A North-country lass to London did pass,
Although with her nature it did not agree.
She did repent and so often lament,
Still wishing again in the North for to be.
Oh, the oak and the ash and the bonny ivy tree
Do flourish at home in my own country."

Playford I
Sharp II 120
Chappell 456

LADY SPELLOR (Easy) 40 Bars

Four-couple longways set

First Verse

A1 Partners take near hands and go up a double and fall back a double. Turn to face eachother, set and turn single.

A2 Repeat A1

Chorus

B1 All turn to face up and take eight small slips to the left (towards the Men's wall); partners face, set and turn single.

B2 Partners fall back a single, then cross over and change places; partners face, set and turn single.

B3 1s, followed by the rest of their lines, take near hands and lead down the middle to the bottom, turn as a couple to their left and lead up back to original places.

Second Verse

A1 Partners side to right shoulders, set and turn single.

A2 Partners side to left shoulders, set and turn single.

B1, 2 & 3 Chorus

Third Verse

A1 Partners arm right, set and turn single.

A2 Partners arm left, set and turn single.

B1, 2 & 3 Chorus

Playford I
Sharp III 75

50

Four-couple longways dance.

First Verse

A1   Partners take near hands, lead up a double and fall back again.

A2   Repeat A1.

B1   1s cast off to the foot, the others following, thus inverting the set; partners set and turn single.

B2   1s cast back up to the top, the others following back to places; partners set and turn single.

Second Verse

A1   Partners side to right shoulders.

A2   Partners side to left shoulders.

B1   All face up; Men slip four small slips to their right, passing in front of their partners who are slipping four slips to their left; partners (now improper) take near hands and lead up a double; partners set and turn single.

A2   All face down; Men slip back to their right, passing behind their partners who are slipping to their left; partners take near hands and lead down a double to places; partners set and turn single.

Third Verse

A1   Partners arm right.

A2   Partners arm left.

B1   1 Man take 2 Woman with two hands and move her up to 1's place while the 3 Man does similar figure with 4 Woman, the 1 and 3 Women stepping out of the way. Then the 2 Man takes the 1 Woman with two hands and moves her down to 2's place while the 4 Man does similar figure with the 3 Woman; then the 1 man changes places with the 2 Man while the 3 Man does the same with the 4 Man by right shoulders. Partners set and turn single.

B2   Repeat B1 back to places with 1 and 3 Men starting; Partners set and turn single. Note: Sharp has changed B1 and B2 to clockwise half-poussettes, set and turn single, a wise change.

The existence of this humorous ditty as a presumably old song at that time was noted in Anthony Munday's *Downfall of Robert, Earl of Huntington* (1597). See Chappell for a more complete text.

"As I lay musing all alone, fa la la la la.
A pretty jest I thought upon, fa la la la la.
Then listen a while and I will tell
Of a friar who loved a bonny lass well,
Fa la la la la, fa la langtre down dilly."

Playford I
Sharp VI 89
Chappell 273

MALL PEATLY   (Moderate-Difficult)   28 Bars

Four-couple longways set

First Verse

A1 Partners take near hands and lead up a double and fall back again.

A2 Repeat A1.

B1 All set to partners; then 1 Man sets to 2 Woman while 4 Man sets to 3 Woman; then 1 Man goes down the set, passing right shoulders with the 4 Man who is coming up the set; the 1 Man goes out between the 3 and 4 Women and does five changes of a hey with them, starting by passing the 4 Woman by the right, while the 4 Man goes out between the 1 and 2 Women and does a similar hey with them, starting by passing left shoulders with the 1 Woman; the 1 Man ends in 4 Man's place and vice versa.

B2 Repeat B1 back to places with 1 and 4 Men reversing roles.

Second Verse

A1 Partners side to right shoulders.

A2 Partners side to left shoulders.

B1 All set to partners; then 1 Woman sets to 2 Man while 4 Woman sets to 3 Man; then 1 and 4 Women do heys with the Men in a mirror image of the heys in B1 of the First Verse.

B2 Repeat B1 back to places with 1 and 4 Women reversing roles.

Third Verse

A1 Partners arm right.

A2 Partners arm left.

B1 All set to partners; then 1 Man sets to 2 Woman while 4 Woman sets to 3 Man; then 1 Man does five changes of a hey with the 2 and 3 Women while 4 Woman does five changes of a hey with the 2 and 3 Men; the 1 Man falls into 4th place proper, the other Men moving up, while the 4 Woman falls into first place proper, the other women moving down.

B2 All set to partners; then 1 Man sets to 2 Woman while 4 Woman sets to 3 Man; then 1 Man does five changes of a hey with the 1 and 2 Women while the 4 Woman does five changes of a hey with the 3 and 4 Men; both end by falling into their original places, the others moving up or down to accommodate them.

The tune was published in Amsterdam in 1622, but with different time signatures. It is believed to be much older. The original words apparently have been lost.

Playford IV
Sharp VI 80
Chappell 289

THE MERRY, MERRY MILKMAIDS (Moderate)

Four-couple longways set.

First Verse

A1 Partners take near hands, lead up a double and fall back again; partners set and turn single.

A2 Repeat A1.

B1 1s take both hands and slip down until they are below the 2s while 3s do likewise with 4s. Both groups do a right-hand star once around.

B2 2s and 4s slip down; both groups do left-hand star once around back to places.

Second Verse

A1 Partners side to right shoulders, set and turn single.

A2 Partners side to left shoulders, set and turn single.

B1 1 Man, followed by the other Men, casts to the foot to invert the set; then the Women do likewise; partners set and turn single.

B2 1 Man, followed by the other Men, casts back up to place; then the Women do likewise; partners set and turn single.

Third Verse

A1 Partners arm right, set and turn single.

A2 Partners arm left, set and turn single.

B1 1 and 3 Men face down and 2 and 4 Men face up; the Men do a straight hey for four, starting by passing right shoulders.

B2 The Women do the figure in B1.

Ophelia, in Shakespeare's *Hamlet*, sang a fragment of the otherwise lost original words of this song:
"And will he not come again? And will he not come again?
No, no, he is dead, gone to his deathbed; he never will come again."
The early seventeenth-century ballad "Keep a good tongue in your head" was set to this tune.

"I married a wife of late, the more's my unhappy fate;
I took her for love as fancy did move, and not for her worldy state.
For qualities rare, few with her compare, let me do her no wrong;
I must confess her chief amiss is only this as some wives' is:
She cannot rule her tongue, she cannot rule her tongue."

During Mary Tudor's reign, Elizabeth was closely guarded and had few opportunities for merriment. Small wonder that upon hearing a milkmaid singing outside the garden Elizabeth said she wished she were a milkmaid, for her life would be better and merrier that way.

Playford I
Sharp III 83
Chappell 237, 295, 777.

MILKMAID'S BOB (Moderate) 16 Bars

Four-couple longways set

First Verse

A1 Partners take near hands and lead up a double and fall back again.

A2 Repeat A1

B1 & 2 1s and 2s do a (slow) circular hey, starting with partners passing by right shoulders, while 3s and 4s do likewise.

Second Verse

A1 Partners side to right shoulders

A2 Partners side to left shoulders

B1 1s slip down between the 2s while the 3s slip between the 4s; partners change places by the right shoulders.

B2 1s slip back up between the 2s while 3s slip between the 4s; partners change places by the right shoulders.

Third Verse

A1 Partners arm right

A2 Partners arm left

A3 (Dividing the set into 2 duple-minor sets), First corners cross by right shoulder; then second corners cross.

A4 First corners cross back; then second corners cross back.

Playford I

Four-couple longways set.
First Verse

A1   Partners take near hands and lead up a double and fall back again.

A2   Repeat A1.

Chorus

B   The top two couples turn to face the Men's wall and take hands with neighbor along the line, while the bottom two couples face the Women's wall. All lead out a double, change hands and lead back to places. Then top two couples face up while bottom two couples face down; partners take near hands and lead forward a double, change hands and lead back a double to places.

C   1 Man, passing in front of the 2 Man, turns the 2 Woman with two hands once around and at the same time the 3 Man passes in front of the 4 Man to turn the 4 Woman, while the 2 Man goes to turn the 1 Woman and the 4 Man goes to turn the 3 Woman. Then, the Men passing by right shoulders turn their partners with two hands once around.

Second Verse

A1   Partners side to right shoulders.

A2   Partners side to left shoulders.

B & C   Chorus

Third Verse

A1   Partners arm right.

A2   Partners arm left.

B & C   Chorus

Chappell states that "The Shepherd's Daughter" was popular in Elizabeth's reign, being "usually printed with her picture before it." In the seventeenth century, it was also known as "Parson and Dorothy," presumably named after the same dancing-master Parson who was responsible for "Parson's Farewell."

"There was a shepherd's daughter
Came tripping on the way
And there by chance a knight she met
Which caused her to stay."

Playford II
Sharp VI 83
Chappell 126

TEN POUND LASS   (Moderate-Difficult)   24 Bars

Four-couple longways set, with bottom two couples improper.

First Verse

A1   Facing partners, take hands along the lines and fall back a double and come forward a double again.
A2   Partners take near hands and lead up a double and fall back again.
B1   All face up and slip eight slips to the left. Then all face partners, cross over and loop into changed places.
B2   All face up and slip eight slips to the right. Then all face partners, cross over and loop into changed places.

Second Verse

A1   Partners side to right shoulders.
A2   Partners side to left shoulders.
B1   The 1s face down while the 4s face up, each taking near hands with partners, and move forward to meet; they circle once around and fall into middle places, while the two middle couples face partners, fall back a double and separate, the 2s slipping up four slips while the 3s slip down four slips, falling into top and bottom places respectively. Then all partners set and turn single.
B2   Repeat B1 with new people back to places.

Third Verse

A1   Partners arm right.
A2   Partners arm left.
B1   Partners cross over and loop around into changed places. Then the dancers in each line, the middle falling back slightly, circle half-way around.
B2   Repeat B1 back to places.

Playford IV
Sharp II 113

Four-couple square or round set

First Verse

A1   All take hands in a ring and slip eight slips clockwise.

A2   All slip back counter-clockwise to places.

B1   1 Man moves in front of his partner to face her; they take both hands and she pushes him back a double towards the middle; then the 2 couple does this figure.

B2   The 3 couple does what the 1s did in B1, then the 4s do this figure. All Men are now in the middle facing out at their partners.

Second Verse

A1   Partners side to right shoulders.

A2   Partners side to left shoulders.

B1   1 Man shakes partner by the right hand three times (on the beats indicated by asterisks in the music) and then changes places with her by a right-hand turn half-way around. Then the 2s do likewise.

B2   The 3s do what the 1s did in B1; then the 4s.

Third Verse

A1   Partners arm right.

A2   Partners arm left.

B1   1 Man taps his partner's right foot with his right foot on the beats indicated by asterisks in the music and then, right hand to right hand, he assists her to move out to her original place. Then the 2s do likewise.

B2   3s do what the 1s did in B1; then the 4s.

This is one of the country dances mentioned in the play *Misogonus* in about 1560.

Playford IV
Sharp III 28
Chappell 84

Four-couple square or round set.

First Verse

A1 Partners take near hands and lead out a double, change hands and lead back a double to places. Each Man gives two hands to his corner and changes places with her. Then the 1 Man change places (using two hands) with the 1 Woman while the 3 Man changes with the 3 Woman, the 2 Man with the 4 Woman and the 4 Man with the 2 Woman.

A2 Men take near hands with the Woman on their right and lead out a double, change hands and lead back a double again. Then each Man changes places with his corner; then the same numbered people who changed at the end of A1 change again, back to places.

B1 Heads lead forward a double and meet and form lines across the set, the 1s with the 4 Man and 2 Woman, the others likewise, and fall back a double. 1 Man arm right with 3 Woman and fall into second place while 3 Man and 1 Woman do likewise into fourth place, 4 Man and 2 Woman to first place and 2 Man and 4 Woman to third place; Women are now standing on Men's left.

B2 Do similar figure to B1 but with 2s and 4s meeting in the middle and all arming by the left to get back to places.

Second Verse

A1 Partners side to right shoulders; then all change places as in A1 of First Verse.

A2 Men side to left shoulders with the Woman on the right, then change places as in A2 of First Verse.

B1 1 Man casts into an eight-step circle around to his right, followed by the 2 Woman, while 3 Man and 4 Woman do likewise, and while 1 Woman makes a circle to her left, followed by the 4 Man, and 3 Woman and 2 Man do likewise. Then 1s circle once around with 4 Man and 2 Woman while others circle as well.

B2 Repeat B1, but with 2s and 4s doing what 1s and 3s did and vice versa.

Third Verse

A1 Partners arm right; then all change places as in First Verse.

A2 All Men arm left with woman on the right and change places as in First Verse.

B1 1s and 3s lead forward and form an outward-facing circle and move that circle once around clockwise, while the 2s and 4s take hands in a ring and circle once around them counter-clockwise. At the end of the circles, 1 Man and 3 Woman fall into second place, 3 Man and 1 Woman into fourth place, 4 Man and 2 Woman into first place and the others to third place.

B2 Repeat B1, but with 2s and 4s doing what 1s and 3s did and vice versa.

The song was well known by 1566 when a parody was registered, and the dance is known to have been popular in 1577.

"Fain I would have a pretie thing to give unto my Ladie;
I name no thing and mean no thing, but as pretty a thing as may be."

Playford I
Sharp III 40
Chappell 91

Four-couple round or square set.

First Verse

A1   All take hands and come forward a double into the middle and fall back again to places; partners set and turn single.

A2   Repeat A1.

B1   The Men move forward a double; then the Women move forward a double while the Men fall back to places. Then, while the Women fall back to places, the Men come forward a double, take hands and go once around clockwise.

B2   Same as B1, except that the Women start the figure and do the circle.

Second Verse

A1   Partners side to right shoulders, set and turn single.

A2   Partners side to left shoulders, set and turn single.

B1   1s and 3s move forward a double; then 2s and 4s move forward a double while 1s and 3s fall back to places. Then, while the 2s and 4s fall back to places, 1s and 3s come forward a double, take hands and go once around clockwise.

B2   Same as B1, except that 2s and 4s start the figure and do the circle.

Third Verse

A1   Partners arm right, set and turn single.

A2   Partners arm left, set and turn single.

B1   The Men go forward a double and turn around, taking hands to form an outward-facing circle and go clockwise once around while the Women skip around them counter-clockwise back to places.

B2   Same as B1, except that the Women start the figure and the Men skip around them.

Playford I
Sharp II 70

HUNSDON HOUSE (Moderate) 40 Bars

Four-couple square set

Chorus

A1 Grand Squares: Heads move forward a double and meet while Sides face partners and fall back a double. 1 Man and 3 Woman take right hand to right hand and fall back into 2s' place while 3 Man and 1 Woman do the same to the 4s' place; at the same time, Sides face their opposites, move forward and meet in the Heads' places; the Women are now to the left of the nearest Men.

A2 (continuation of Grand Squares) 2s and 4s move forward and meet while 1s and 3s fall back; 2s and 4s take right hand to right hand and fall back to original places while 1s and 3s face partners and move forward to meet in original places.

First Verse

B1 Heads move forward a double, meet and do a cloverleaf turn single; then 1 and 3 Men cross over by right shoulders and fall back into eachother's places; then 1 and 3 Women do the same.

B2 Side couples do the figure in B1.

B3 Heads repeat B1 back to places.

B4 Sides repeat B2 back to places.

Second Verse

A1 & 2 Chorus.

B1 Heads move forward a double, Men turning clockwise and Women turning counter-clockwise so as to form an outward-facing circle. Take hands, go half-way around clockwise and move out to opposite places.

B2 Sides do the figure in B1.

B3 Heads repeat B1 back to places.

B4 Sides repeat B2 back to places.

Third Verse

A1 & 2 Chorus.

B1 Heads move forward a double and meet; partners honour; then two changes of a circular hey with hands, starting by giving right to opposites, and fall into opposite places.

B2 Sides do figure in B1.

B3 Heads move forward a double and meet; opposites honour; then two changes of a circular hey, starting by giving right hands to partners and fall back to original places.

B4 Sides do figure in B3.

This dance is the earliest surviving example of a square dance whose directions were written down, in this case on a manuscript of 1648 from the Inns of Court. Henry Carey, first Lord Hunsdon, was Queen Elizabeth's Lord Chamberlain, and she made a great show of visiting him at his country estate, Hunsdon House, both in 1571 and in 1580. It is likely that the dance can be dated to one or other of those years. Hunsdon House, in Hertfordshire, still stands in much altered state.

Playford III
Sharp III 47

HYDE PARK (Moderate) 24 Bars

Four-couple square set.

Chorus

A1 Heads lead forward a double, meet and fall back to places.

A2 Sides lead forward a double, meet and fall back to places.

First Verse

B1 Heads face partners, fall back a single, come forward a single, take both hands and slip into the middle and meet. 1 Man takes both hands with 3 Woman and they slip out between the 2s, then separate and cast back to places, while 3 Man and 1 Woman do likewise between the 4s.

B2 Sides do similar figure to B1.

Second Verse

A1 & 2 Chorus.

B1 Sides turn partners half-way around with right hands and make an arch with right hands; Heads face partners and pass by right shoulders as they skip one-quarter of the way around the outside of the set and enter through the arches, returning to partners' places.

B2 Heads do what Sides did in B1 and vice versa until all are back at original places.

Third Verse

A1 & 2 Chorus.

B1 Men face counter-clockwise and weave a ring through the Women using a skipping step, and starting by passing partners by right shoulders (Some irreverent dancers call this "The Grand Leer").

B2 Women face clockwise and weave a ring through the Men, using a skipping step, and starting by passing partners by left shoulders.

Hyde Park was the name of a play written in London in 1632 by James Shirley (1596-1666), but the dance seems to be older than this and is probably named directly for one of London's most beautiful parks that was even popular in the sixteenth century. The Hyde/Clarendon family served the Tudors and Stuarts for many generations.

Playford I
Sharp III 44

Four-couple square set

First Verse

A1   All take near hands and move forward a double into the center and fall back a double to places; set to partners and turn single.

A2   Repeat A1

A3   Head Men change places; then Head Women change places; Heads face partners and do two changes of a circular hey with hands back to original places.

A4   Side couples do the figure in A3.

Second Verse

A1   Partners side to right shoulders, set and turn single.

A2   Partners side to left shoulders, set and turn single.

A3   Heads lead forward a double and meet; 1 Man leads 3 Woman out between the 2s, separate and cast skipping back to places while the others do likewise between the 4s; Heads turn partners once around with two hands.

A4   Sides do the figure in A3.

Third Verse

A1   Partners arm right; set and turn single.

A2   Partners arm left; set and turn single.

A3   1 Man and 3 Woman change places, while 3 Man and 1 Woman do likewise; Head partners change by right shoulders; Heads, facing across the set, do two changes of a circular hey with hands, starting by right hands with one's opposite.

A4   Side couples do the figure in A3.

This tune and dance take their name from the old children's rhyme:

If all the world were paper and all the water ink,
If all the trees were bread and cheese,
What would I have to drink?

Playford I
Sharp III 30

62

MAGE ON A CREE   (Moderate)   32 Bars

Honours   A1   A2   A3   A4

Four-couple square set

First Verse

A1 All take hands and move into the center a double and fall back a double to places. Partners face eachother, set and turn single.

A2 Repeat A1

A3 Head Men go into the center and stand back to back; then the Side Men do the same. Each man turns his corner once around with two hands.

A4 The Women do the same figure as in A3, except they turn their partners.

Second Verse

A1 Partners side to right shoulders, set and turn single.

A2 Partners side to left shoulders, set and turn single.

A3 Men skip a weaving figure half way around clockwise, passing the corner by left shoulder. Then Women move forward a double into the center and fall back a double to places, turning single as they go.

A4 Repeat A3 back to places.

Third Verse

A1 Partners arm right, set and turn single.

A2 Partners arm left, set and turn single.

A3 Using a skipping step, each Man turns the Woman on his left with two hands once and a half around; each Man then does the same with the next Woman on his left. Note: the Women are not to move out of their places, so the Men make the extra effort to travel around the set.

A4 Repeat A3 around to places.

According to the *Oxford English Dictionary*, Mage on a Cree means Wise-man (as in Magi) at the bursting point.

Playford I
Sharp II 68

Four-couple round set.

First Verse

A1 All take hands and slip eight slips clockwise.

A2 Slip eight slips counter-clockwise back to places.

B1 Partners set and turn single.

B2 Corners set and turn single.

Second Verse

A1 Heads partners join hands and make an arch for the Side Man on the right, who moves forward a double and goes under the arch; Heads still holding hands do a turn half-way around counter-clockwise while the Side Men turn to face them.

A2 Repeat A1 back to places.

B1 Partners set and turn single.

B2 Corners set and turn single.

Third Verse

Repeat Second Verse with Sides making arches for Head Man on the right.

Fourth Verse

A1 1 and 4 Men make an arch facing outwards at the 1 Woman while 3 and 2 Men do likewise with the 3 Woman. The Women go under the arch and turn about to face the arch while the Men arm right half way around.

A2 Repeat A1 back to places, the Men arming left.

B1 Partners set and turn single.

B2 Corners set and turn single.

Fifth Verse

Repeat Fourth Verse with Men making arches for Side Woman on the right.

Sixth Verse

A1 4 Man and 1 Woman make an arch for the 1 Man while the 2 Man and 3 Woman do the same for the 3 Man. After the Head Men have gone through their arch, the people making the arches turn half-way around clockwise.

A2 Repeat A1 back to places.

B1 Partners set and turn single.

B2 Corners set and turn single.

Seventh Verse

Repeat Sixth Verse with 1 Man and 2 Woman making an arch for the 2 Man and 3 Man and 4 Woman making an arch for the 4 Man.

The tune was well known in 1581 when new words were set to it about the discovery of a plot against the boy King James VI of Scotland.

"Out, alas, what grief is this that princes' subjects can not be true.
But still the Devil hath some of his to play their parts whate'er ensue,
Forgetting what a grievous thing it is to offend the annointed king.
Alas, for woe, why should it be so? This makes a sorrowful heigh-ho."

This is a slightly simplified arrangement of the rather tedious instructions for the dance in Playford.

Playford I
Sharp VI 56
Chappell 185

Four-couple round or square set.

First Verse

A1 All take hands, come forward a double and fall back a double to places; partners set to eachother, then corners set to eachother.

A2 Repeat A1.

B1 Partners arm right, ending with Men doing a left-hand star once around while the Women skip around them clockwise.

B2 Partners arm left, ending with Women doing a right-hand star once around while the men skip around them counter-clockwise.

Second Verse

A1 Partners side to right shoulders; take a single to the right and honour and then on to the next person in the direction one is facing.

A2 Side to left shoulders with the new person; take a single to the right and honour and then on to the next person.

B1 Heads (now in Sides' places, 1 Man with 3 Woman and 3 Man with 1 Woman) take near hands, lead into the middle a double, change hands and lead out a single and make an arch. Side people separate, cast around the outside one quarter of the way around and go through the arches and return to the same places.

B2 Repeat B1 with Sides making the arches and Heads going through them.

Third Verse

A1 Present "partners" arm right, then arm left and then move on to the next person (Men continuing to go counter-clockwise and Women clockwise).

A2 Arm right with the next, then arm left, giving an extra "flip" to put the Woman on the Man's right and form lines of four arranged longways, the 2s joining hands with 1 Man and 3 Woman and the 4s with 3 Man and 1 Woman. Keep the lines straight and close together.

B1 The lines fall back a double and come forward a double. All turn single. Then each Man changes places by right shoulders with the Woman in front of him; however, as the lines pass through, they are dissolved to be re-formed into new lines going across the set, the 1s joining hands with 2 Man and 4 Woman, and the 3s with 4 Man and 2 Woman. Those who were on the ends of the previous lines are in the middle of these lines and vice versa. Keep the lines straight and close together.

B2 The lines fall back a double and come forward a double. All turn single. Then each Man changes places by right shoulders with the Woman in front of him, and all end up in a square set with original partners in original positions—magic!

The tune was probably already old when it was used in *Friar Bacon*, written some time before 1592.

"O come you from Newcastle? Come you not there away?
O met you not my true love, riding on a bonny bay?
To couple is a custome, all things thereto agree;
Why should not I then love, since love to all is free?"

Playford I
Sharp II 72
Chappell 340, 779

NEWCASTLE OLD (Easy-Moderate)

Newcastle, as given in this book and by Playford, exudes a strong feeling that it was once a simpler dance that was subsequently rewritten in a more complicated form for show. Therefore, at the risk of enraging the many loyal fans of the standard Newcastle, the author is here presenting his attempt at reconstructing the Elizabethan dance as it may have been before it was altered by the seventeenth-century dancing-master(s).

First Verse (unchanged)

A1 All take hands, come forward a double and fall back a double to places. Partners set to eachother, then corners set to eachother.

A2 Repeat A1

B1 Partners arm right, ending with Men doing a left-hand star once around while the Women skip around them clockwise.

B2 Partners arm left, ending with Women doing a right-hand star once around while the Men skip around them counter-clockwise.

Second Verse

A1 Partners side to right shoulders. Partners set to eachother, then corners set to eachother.

A2 Repeat A1, siding to left shoulder.

B1 Head partners take near hands and lead forward a double, change hands and lead back out a single and make an arch. Side people separate, cast off and go through the arches and all return to original places.

B2 Repeat B1 with sides making the arches and Heads going through them.

Third Verse

A1 Partners arm right. Partners set to eachother, then corners set to eachother.

A2 Repeat A1, arming left, but end with the set arranged in lines of 4 *longways*.

B1 The lines, which should start out close together, take hands and fall back a double and then come forward a double. All couples do a 2-hand turn once around with partners, and end the turns in lines of 4 *across the set*, the Side couples at the ends.

B2 Repeat B1, and end the dance back in the square set.

OAKEN LEAVES   (Moderate)   32 Bars

Four-couple circular or square set.

First Verse

A1 All take hands and slip eight slips clockwise; partners set and turn single.

A2 All take hands and slip eight slips counter-clockwise; partners set and turn single.

A3 1 and 2 Men change places; then 1 and 2 Women changes places (by right shoulders each time). Then 1 and 2 couples do two changes of a circular hey back to places, starting with partners passing by right shoulders.

A4 A3 is repeated by 3 and 4 couples.

A5 A3 is repeated by 1 and 4 couples.

A6 A3 is repeated by 2 and 3 couples.

Second Verse

A1 Partners side to right shoulders, set and turn single.

A2 Partners side to left shoulders, set and turn single.

A3 Partners take near hands and lead out a double, change hands and lead back again. Each Man, passing his partner by right shoulders, turns the next Woman on his right with two hands once around clockwise and falls into her partner's place.

A4-6 The figure in A3 is repeated with new partners until all are back in original places.

Third Verse

A1 Partners arm right, set and turn single.

A2 Partners arm left, set and turn single.

A3 The Men move forward a double into the center and fall back again to places. Each man then turns the Woman on his left once and a half around with two hands and moves into her partners place, the Woman taking care that she does not move out of her place while the Man travels around the set clockwise.

A4-6 The figure in A3 is repeated with new partners until all are back in original places.

Sharp does not supply the original tune for this dance, although it is shown here.

Playford IV
Sharp IV 38

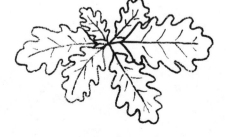

ORANGES & LEMONS (Moderate-Difficult) 32 Bars

Four-couple square set

First Verse

A1 All take hands and move forward a double and fall back again.

A2 Repeat A1.

B1 & 2 Partners honour; then corners honour; then the Men circle half way around clockwise and fall back into opposite places. New corners honour; then new partners honour, then the Women circle half way around clockwise and fall in beside their original partners.

B3 & 4 Repeat B1 & 2 back to places.

Second Verse

A1 Partners side to right shoulders

A2 Partners side to left shoulders

B1 & 2 Partners take right hand to right hand and move a single to the right, then left hand to left hand and move a single to the left. Then do two changes of a circular hey, starting by passing partners by right shoulders. Then repeat the whole of this figure with the next people.

B3 & 4 Repeat B1 & 2 back to original places.

Third Verse

A1 Partners arm right.

A2 Partners arm left

B1 & 2 Forming a diagonal axis through the set, the 1 and 2 couples honour their opposites while the 3 and 4 couples do the same; then partners honour; then the 1 and 2 couples circle half way around and fall back into eachother's places, while the 3 and 4 couples do the same. Next, forming the other diagonal axis through the set, the 1 and 4 couples repeat this whole figure while the 2 and 3 couples do likewise.

B3 & 3 Repeat the figures in B1 & 2 until all are back in original places.

The old nursery rhyme

' "Oranges & Lemons,"
Say the bells of St. Clement's . . .'

is of course not to this tune, nor should it be, because it simply refers to the fact that the bells of St. Clement-Danes (which is close to the Inns of Court where Oranges & Lemons was often danced) are reflecting the dance tune.

Playford III
Sharp II 79

PEPPERS BLACK   (Difficult)   16 Bars

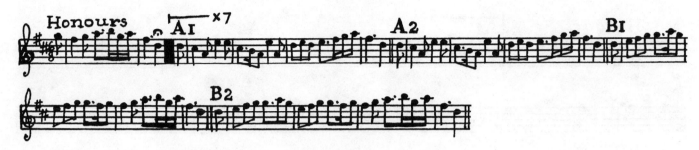

Four-couple square or round set.

First Verse

A1 All take hands and slip eight slips clockwise.
A2 Slip eight slips counter-clockwise back to places.
B1 Partners set and turn single.
B2 Corners set and turn single.

Second Verse

A1 Head couples take near hands and lead forward a double over to the Side couple on the left, and fall back to places again.
A2 Side couples do the same to the Heads on their right.
B1 1 Man turns the 2 Woman once around with two hands while the 2 Man and 1 Woman do the same, the 3 Man and 4 Woman do the same and the 4 Man and 3 Woman do the same.
B2 Partners turn once around with two hands.

Third Verse

Head couples repeat Second Verse with Sides on their right.

Fourth Verse

A1 Repeat A1 of Second Verse.
A2 Repeat A2 of Second Verse.
B1 & 2 Those couples do four changes of a circular hey starting by passing opposites by right shoulders, and come back to places.

Fifth Verse

Heads repeat Fourth Verse with Sides on their right.

Sixth Verse

A1 Heads take near hands with partners and lead forward a double; each Head Man takes in his left hand the right hand of the Side Man to his left, and together all three fall back a double to the 1s' place.
A2 The three of them lead forward a double to the Side Woman and fall back again.
B1 The same Men raise their hands and make an arch; the Head Men turn around once counter-clockwise on that axis, bringing the Head Women under the arch and back to places.
B2 The Head partners now make an arch; the Head Men then turn once around clockwise on that axis, bringing the Side Man under the arch and propelling him behind his partner and back to place.

Seventh Verse

Sides repeat Sixth Verse with Heads on their left.

This is a slightly simplified arrangement of the rather tedious instructions in Playford. The dance was mentioned in 1596. The original words are lost, but a subsequent set of words appeared before 1600:

"Look up, my lords, and mark my words
And hear what I shall sing ye;
And subjects all, both great and small,
now mark what words I bring ye."

For some reason, Sharp used a different tune, but the original is given here.

Playford I
Sharp VI 54
Chappell 121

ROSE IS WHITE AND ROSE IS RED   (Moderate)   32 Bars

Four-couple square set (originally round for as many as will)

First Verse

A1 All take near hands and lead into the center a double and fall back again, face partner, set and turn single.
A2 Repeat A1
A3 Side couples lead forward a double to the couple on their right and fall back a double. Side couples then circle once around with the Head Men (in separate circles)
A4 Side couples repeat A3 with Head Women.

Second Verse

A1 Partners side to right shoulders, set and turn single.
A2 Partners side to left shoulders, set and turn single.
A3 Head couples lead forward a double to the couple on their right and fall back a double. Head couples and Side Men do a straight hey (beginning with Side Man passing Head Woman by right shoulders)
A4 Head couples repeat A3 with Side Woman.

Third Verse

A1 Partners arm right, set and turn single
A2 Partners arm left, set and turn single
A3 Side couples each make an arch and move forward a double towards the Head Man on their right who moves forward a double and passes under the arch. All three turn about and repeat the figure in the opposite direction. Then all partners turn once around with two hands.
A4 Side couples repeat A3 with Head Women.

This dance has been shortened to avoid needless repetitions.

Playford I
Sharp VI 52

SAGE LEAF   (Easy-Moderate)   40 Bars

Four-couple round or square set

First Verse

A1 All take hands and slip eight slips clockwise.
A2 All take hands and slip eight slips counter-clockwise.

Chorus

B   The Men come forward into the centre a double and fall back again. Then the Women do likewise.
C   All take hands and come forward a double into the center and fall back again. Then partners turn with the right hand once around.
D1-4 Each couple turn with two hands once and a half around clockwise, and the figure is repeated with the next three people until all are back in original places. In the first and third verses, the Men travels thus around the set while the Women remain in their original places throughout all the turns, but in the second verse the Women travel around the set (clockwise) while the Men hold their places.

Second Verse

A1 Partners side to right shoulders.
A2 Partners side to left shoulders.

B-D4 Chorus.

Third Verse

A1 Partners arm right.
A2 Partners arm left.

B-D4 Chorus.

The Playford directions for this dance are somewhat garbled, and this interpretation of them is at odds with Sharp's. The original dance was for a circle for as many as will, but the dance's duration is more manageable for four couples.

Playford IV
Sharp VI 58

Four-couple square or round set.

First Verse

A1　All take hands and lead forward a double into the middle and fall back again; partners set and turn single.

A2　Repeat A1.

Second Verse

A1　Head partners take near hands and lead between the Side couple on their left, separate and cast off around the Side couple and meet again in front of the Sides. All clap hands once; then partners arm right, ending facing across the set with Woman on the right.

A2　Heads pass eachother, right shoulder to right shoulder, until they arrive in front of the other Side couple; they lead between the Side couple, separate and cast off and meet in front of the Sides. All clap hands once; then partners arm right and return to places.

Third Verse

A1 & 2　Repeat the Second Verse, substituting a right-hand star once around for "arm right."

Fourth Verse

A1 & 2　Repeat the Second Verse, substituting circle four-hands once around clockwise for "arm right."

Ben Jonson mentioned this tune in 1599, and Robert Herrick wrote no fewer than six new songs to this same tune about 1620, some of which apparently follow the pattern of the original, whose verses often ended with the words "Up tails all" on the last three notes. A slightly simplified arrangement of the rather tedious dance instructions given in Playford is offered here.

Playford I
Sharp III
Chappell 196, 773

Four-couple round or square set (formerly round for as many as will)

First Verse

A1   All take hands and slip eight slips clockwise, then turn single.
A2   Slip back eight slips counter-clockwise, then turn single.

Chorus

A3-6   The Men move forward a double to the center and fall back again to places. Then each man passes the woman on his left by right shoulders and arrives in the next man's place. This figure is repeated until all the men have travelled completely around the set clockwise. The chorus for the second verse differs in that it is the Women who are active, and they pass the men by left shoulders going counter-clockwise.

Second Verse

A1   Partners side to right shoulders, then turn single.
A2   Partners side to left shoulders, then turn single.
A3-6   Women's chorus.

Third Verse

A1   Partners arm right, then turn single.
A2   Partners arm left, then turn single.
A3-6   Men's chorus.

This interpretation shortens the dance somewhat by eliminating tedious repeats.

Playford II
Sharp III 34

DARGASON/THE SEDANNY   (Easy-Moderate)   8 Bars

Circular set for as many as will, but also danced in a single-line longways set with all the Men on one end facing towards the Women's end. The dance is more difficult and can become tedious in the longways formation, so the circle is taught here. The longways form is almost certainly later, for indoors.

First Verse

A1   All take hands in a ring and slip eight slips clockwise; partners set and turn single.

A2   Slip eight slips counter-clockwise back to places; partners set and turn single.

Second Verse

A1   Partners side to right shoulders, set and pass eachother by right shoulders, turning single as they go; they face the next person.

A2 & c.   This figure is repeated until partners meet eachother at the opposite side of the set, at which time the dancers begin siding to left shoulders and passing eachother by left shoulders until they are back to places. The music is played as many times as needed.

Third Verse

A1   Partners arm right, set and pass eachother by right shoulders, turning single as they go; they then face the next person.

A2 & c.   This figure is repeated with the next people until partners meet eachother at the opposite side of the set, at which time the dancers begin to arm left and pass eachother by left shoulders until they are back to places.

Fourth Verse

A1 & c.   Circular hey completely around the set, starting with partners passing by right shoulders; a skipping step is appropriate.

"Dargason" is believed to be one of the oldest surviving English dances, going back to a period at least before the Reformation. The tune will be recognized by some dancers as an earlier form of the eighteenth-century dance tune "The Irish Washerwoman." Chappell gives at least three sets of words to "Dargason," all of uncertain age, of which one, called "The Shropshire Wakes" or "Hey for Christmas," contains allusions to dancing.

"Come Robin, Ralph and little Harry
And merry Thomas to our green,
Where we shall meet with Bridget and Sary
And the finest girls that e'er were seen.
Then hey for Christmas once a year,
When we have cakes with ale and beer,
For at Christmas every day
Young men and maids may dance away . . ."

Playford I
Sharp II 118
Chappell 63

EPPING FOREST   (Easy)   32 Bars

Circular set for as many as will.

First Verse

A1 All take hands in a ring and slip eight slips clockwise; partners set and turn single.
A2 Slip eight slips counter-clockwise back to places; partners set and turn single.

Chorus

B Partners slow set to the right and honour, then slow set to the left and honour. Then corners slow set to the right and honour, then slow set to the left and honour.
C Partners do a two-hand turn (either walking or skipping step). Then corners do a two-hand turn.

Second Verse

A1 Partners side to right shoulders, set and turn single.
A2 Partners side to left shoulders, set and turn single.
B & C   Chorus.

Third Verse

A1 Partners arm right, set and turn single.
A2 Partners arm left, set and turn single.
B & C   Chorus.

Although Playford and Sharp state that this dance is for three couples in a circle, it actually does not matter how many couples form the set.

Playford IV
Sharp VI 64

76

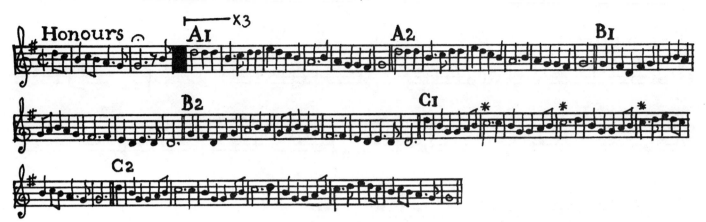

Circle for as Many as Will

First Verse

A1   All take hands and slip eight slips clockwise; all turn single.

A2   Slip eight slips counter-clockwise to places; all turn single.

Chorus

B1   Men, stepping in towards the middle, take hands in a ring and slip clockwise around the circle and fall into convenient places (for sets of 4 to 6 couples, convenient places should be original places)

B2   Women do likewise, falling into place on their partners' right.

C1   Men come forward a single and clap on the beat indicated by an astcrisk in the music; while the Men fall back, the Women come forward a single and clap on the beat indicated by the second asterisk; while the Women fall back, the Men come forward a single and clap on the beat indicated by the third asterisk, and then turn single as they return to places.

C2   Women go in and clap; Men go in and clap; Women go in and clap and turn single back to places.

Second Verse

A1   Partners side to right shoulders, then turn single.

A2   Partners side to left shoulders, then turn single.

B-C   Chorus (starting with the Women this time).

Third Verse

A1   Partners arm right, then turn single.

A2   Partners arm left, then turn single.

B-C   Chorus (starting with the Men).

This is believed to be one of the oldest surviving English dances. Although it is described by Playford as being intended for "as many as will," the B figures will not comfortably bring the dancers back to their original places unless the set is limited to four or possibly five couples.

Playford I
Sharp II 76
Chappell 258, 627

Circular set for as many as will, Women on partner's right.

A1   All take near hands and lead in a double and fall back a double to places.
A2   Repeat A1.
B1   Partners side to right shoulders, then side to left shoulders.
B2   Partners arm right once around, then arm left 1½ times around. Each Man should now have a new Woman on his right with whom to begin the next verse of the dance.

Playford describes this as a longways dance, and it can be danced that way (especially with the odd-numbered couples improper), but it seems better suited to a circular set. A certain amount of reconstruction has had to be done, as Playford's version seems to have been altered and left incomplete.

This tune, very characteristic of traditional Italian shepherd music, was apparently in use in England by 1537, when it was known as Hankin Boby (*sic* Hannikin Booby) in the play *Thersytes*. It was also sometimes known as Hanskin. In *The Dramatic Records of Sir Henry Herbert* (1623, published 1917), Huff Hamukin and The Soldiers of March are listed as country dances of the period.

Playford I
Sharp IV 69
Chappell 73

Circular set for as many as will

First Verse

A   All take hands and slip eight slips clockwise; then slip eight slips counterclockwise back to places.

B   Partners face, set and turn single, then set and turn single again.

Chorus

C   Starting with partners facing, and passing by right shoulders, all do a hey, alternating with right and left shoulders, eight changes. If dancers finish with new partners for the next verse (as they will unless the set is exactly eight couples) it is no cause for alarm.

Second Verse

A   Partners side to right shoulders and then side to left shoulders.

B   Partners face, set and turn single, twice.

C   Chorus.

Third Verse

A   Partners arm right and then arm left.

B   Partners face, set and turn single, twice.

C   Chorus.

There are more mentions of Hey de Gie in early literature than of any other dance, but no English source preserves either the music or the dance directions. However, many experts feel that this is the dance that Arbeau offers in variant form under the name of La Dance de la Haye in *Orchesographie*, and so an attempt has been made here to reconstruct it according to English principles.

Orchesographie, 1588

NOEL   (Easy-Moderate)   24 Bars

Circle for as Many as Will

First Verse

A1   All take hands and slip left eight slips.
A2   Slip back to the right to places.

Chorus

B1   All the Men take hands and slip a circle to the left for 12 slips and fall back into convenient places; each Man
      and the Woman on his right turn to face while the Women step to the right and honour.*
B2   All the Women take hands and slip 12 slips to the left and fall back on their partners' right. Partners turn to
      face, and the Men take a step to the right and honour.*

Second Verse

A1   Partners side to right shoulders.
A2   Partners side to left shoulders.
B1 & 2   Chorus.

Third Verse

A1   Partners arm right.
A2   Partners arm left.
B1 & 2   Chorus.

* The original instructions called for the slipping figure to end with the Man grasping his partner by the waist and lifting her in the air; however, for most occasions the step and honour should be more appropriate.

This jolly dance is not in Playford at all, and since it is only known from a French book of 1588 it is entirely possible that it was never danced in England, although the book was known in England almost as soon as it was
published. English-speaking people will recognise the tune as belonging to the Christmas carol "Ding, dong,
merrily on high," whose words are by George Woodward, © the Society for the Promotion of Christian
Knowledge.

from *Orchesographie*,
1588.

80

Round set for as many as will.

First Verse

A1   All take hands in a ring and slip eight slips clockwise.

A2   Slip eight slips counter-clockwise back to places.

Chorus

B1   Partners (only) take near hands and come forward towards the middle using a setting step and fall back a double to places. Then partners set and turn single.

B2   Repeat B1.

Second Verse

A1   Partners side to right shoulders.

A2   Partners side to left shoulders.

B1 & 2   Chorus.

Third Verse

A1   Partners arm right.

A2   Partners arm left.

B1 & 2   Chorus.

Henry VIII

Fourth Verse (not in Playford)

A1 & 2   Circular hey (eight bars) around with a skipping step, starting by passing partners by the right.

B1 & 2   Chorus.

Playford gave only the first three verses, but Chappell cites a seventeenth-century woodcut showing people dancing in a circle entitled "Hey for Sellenger's Round," implying an extra verse devoted to the hey. The woodcut has since been lost. Playford gave a new tune, but Sharp replaced that with the original tune; Playford, in his later editions, added an extra verse between the First and Second (take hands and all dance a double into the middle and back). Strangely enough, the first listing of this dance in Playford shows it to have been danced as a three-couple longways set at that time.

The tune is ancient, being derived from the same source as the tune for the well-known Palm Sunday hymn "All glory, laud and honour," thought to date from the fifteenth century. Chappell thought it was named after Sir Thomas Sellynger (died before 1475) or perhaps after Sir Antony St. Leger, Henry VIII's Lord Deputy of Ireland in 1540. It is mentioned as a popular dance in many late sixteenth-century documents. The alternate title refers to a song set to the old tune late in Elizabeth's reign.

Playford IV
Sharp IV 40
Chappell 69

Non-progressive longways set for as many as will.

First Verse

A1   Partners take near hands and lead up a double and fall back again.

A2   Repeat A1.

Chorus

B1   1 Man (top man only) faces down and moves a single backwards. Then he dances down the middle and does a counter-clockwise two-hand turn with a skipping step with the last-but-one Woman, followed by a clockwise turn with the last Woman, while the 2 Man leads the rest of the Men with a skipping step between the 1 and 2 Women, casts up to the left and down the Men's side to invert the set, where they find the 1 Man falling into bottom place.

B2   1 Man (at the foot) faces up and moves a single backwards. Then he dances up the middle and does a clockwise two-hand turn with a skipping step with the 2 Woman, followed by a counter-clockwise turn with the 1 Woman, while the 2 Man leads the rest of the Men with a skipping step between the bottom two Women and casts down to the right and up the Men's line to places, where they find the 1 Man has fallen into his original place.

Second Verse

A1   Partners side to right shoulders.

A2   Partners side to left shoulders.

B1 & 2   Chorus: mirror-image of Chorus of First Verse, with the Women doing what the Men did.

Third Verse

A1   Partners arm right.

A2   Partners arm left.

B1 & 2   Chorus (Men active again).

Chappellsays this is an Elizabethan tune, and he gives no fewer than twelve verses for a Christmas song set to the tune:

"All hail to the days that merit more praise than all the rest of the year
And welcome the nights that double delights as well for the poor as the peer.
Good fortune attend each merry man's friend that doth but the best that he may,
Forgetting old wrongs with carols and songs, to drive the cold winter away."

Playford I
Sharp VI 91
Chappell 193

Non-progressive   Longways set for as many as will

First Verse

A1   Partners take near hands and lead up a double and fall back again.

A2   Repeat A1

Chorus

B1   Still facing up, Women slip right a double. Then the Men walk a double over to their partners who turn their backs on them. Each man stands behind his partner with his hands on her shoulders and peep over her right shoulder at the place marked with an asterisk in the music, then her left shoulder, then her right shoulder, then her left shoulder. Then, all face up and slip left four slips. All turn single.

B2   Repeat B2 on the Men's side with Women doing the peeping (if they can reach that high).

Second Verse

A1   Partners side to right shoulders

A2   Partners side to left shoulders

B1 & 2   Chorus (Men's side first this time)

Third Verse

A1   Partners arm right

A2   Partners arm left

B1 & 2   Chorus (Women's side first).

Playford I
Sharp II 123

STANES MORRIS   (Moderate)   20 Bars

Progressive longways for as many as will.   Note: it is best to have short sets of four to six couples.

First Verse

A1   Partners take near hands and lead up a double and fall back again.
A2   Repeat A1.
B1   All face the Men's wall and move forward a double (without hands).
B2   All fall back a double to places; partners face eachother.
C1   Partners set and turn single.
C2   Partners set and turn single.

Second Verse (progressive)

A1   1 Man dances down the middle to stand in front of the last Woman.
A2   1 Man and last Woman side to right shoulders.
B1   1 Man and last Woman do right-hand turn half way around.
B2   1 Man and last Woman do left-hand turn half-way around.
C1   1 Man and last Woman do a two-hand turn clockwise half-way around and then counter-clockwise half-way around.
C2   1 Man and last Woman take two hands and slip up to the top of the set while rest of Women move down one place; last Woman falls into top place in Women's line while 1 Man casts quickly to last place in the Men's line, the rest of the Men moving up one place.

The whole dance is repeated until the original 1 Man is back in his original place.

This jolly tune, which first appears in William Ballet's Lute Book (Elizabethan), apparently has absolutely nothing to do with the town of Staines, near London, but is thought to have a connection with tin-mining areas of England, which were known as the Stannaries (Sir Walter Ralegh was appointed Lord Warden of the Stannaries).

The interpretation of the dance given here seems closer to Playford's garbled original than Sharp's version.

Chappell cleverly took the slightly later words of the Maypole Song in *Actaeon and Diana* and set them to this tune, an arrangement that is felicitous and universally accepted.

"Come, ye young men, come along
With your music and your song.
Bring your lasses in your hands,
For 'tis that which love commands
Then to the Maypole haste away
For 'tis now our holiday."

Playford I
Sharp II 125
Chappell 125

Progressive longways set for as many as will.

First Verse

A   Partners take near hands and lead up a double and fall back again; Repeat.
B   Top couple, followed by the rest of the dancers, cast off to the bottom of the set and lead up the middle back to places.

Second Verse

AB, etc. All join near hands with partners and do a progressive, arched hey, thus: 1s go under the arch made by the 2s, make an arch for the 3s, go under the 4s, etc.; each couple begins the hey when the 1s reach them. Couples reaching either end of the set reverse direction, and the hey continues until all are back in original places.

Third Verse

AB, etc. 1 Man arms right with partner, then arm left with 2 Woman, arm right again with partner, arm left with 3 Woman, etc., while 1 Woman arms left with the various Men alternating with arming right with partner. Playford's instructions call for this figure to continue back up to the top again after the 1s reach the foot, but it would make a more interesting dance if the 1s remained at the foot and all began the dance over again with a new top couple. Playford also suggests repeating the Third Verse (with the same top couple active) once with right-hand and left-hand turns replacing the arm right and arm left, and again with setting to partner and setting to the next opposite replacing arm right and arm left, but it is probably best to omit these extra verses, or else the dancers will spend all evening on this one dance!

By 1564, when it was mentioned in a play by William Bulleyn, "Trenchmore" was already a well-known dance. Surprisingly, its directions were not published until 1721. Describing Elizabethan evenings of dancing in *Table Talk*, the early seventeenth-century revolutionary John Selden says: "At a solemn dancing, first you had the grave Measures, then the Corantoes and Galliards, and this kept up with ceremony; and at length to Trenchmore and the Cushion Dance; then all the company dances [together], lord and groom, lady and kitchen maid, no distinction." Thomas Ravenscroft says in *Deuteromelia* (1609) that this tune was sung in Henry VIII's reign with these words:

"Tomorrow the fox will come to town, keep keep keep keep;
Tomorrow the fox will come to town, o keep you all well there.
Halloo the fox out of the hall and cry as loud as you can call:
'Whoop whoop whoop whoop,'
And cry as loud as you can call, o keep you all well there."

Trenchmore survived in altered form to our own day, known as the Virginia Reel in America and Sir Roger de Coverley in England.

Playford Vol. I, 1721
Country Dance Book,
New Series 6
Chappell 82, 769

Progressive   Longways duple-minor set for as many as will.

First verse repeated until top couple reach the foot.

A1   Partners take near hands and lead up a double and fall back again.
A2   Repeat A1.
B   1s fall back a single, come forward and change places taking right hands; then the 1s take two hands and slip down into second place and change places while the 2s move up.

Second Verse repeated until new top couple reach the foot.

A1   Partners side to right shoulders.
A2   Partners side to left shoulders.
B   The 2s cast up the outside to 1s' places while the 1s cross over as they move down into the 2s' places; then 1s cross back to their own sides. Then the 2s, followed by the 1s, cast off in a circle and all return to their progressed places.

Third Verse repeated until top couple reach the foot.

A1   Partners arm right.
A2   Partners arm left.
B   The 1s cast off below the 2s and return up the middle to places. Then the 1s take both hands and slip four short slips down the middle to second places while the 2s move up the outside into first places; then all turn single (cloverleaf).

Playford IV
Sharp III 93

86

THE FIT'S UPON ME NOW   (Moderate)   16 Bars

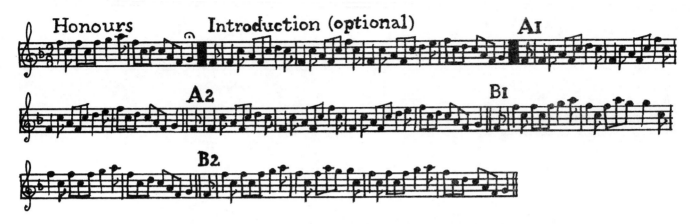

Duple-minor progressive longways dance for as many as will

Introduction (optional)

Partners take near hands and lead up three steps and fall back again to places; repeat.

The Dance

A1 1 Man casts down below the 2 Man and back up the middle to place, while the 2 Woman dances up the middle and casts off around the 1 Woman and back to place. Partners turn once around with two hands.

A2 1 Woman casts down below 2 Woman and back up the middle to place, while the 2 man dances up the middle, casts off around the 1 Man and back to place; partners turn once around with two hands.

B1 2s cross over by right shoulders and change places while the 1s do a back-to-back. Then 1s dance down between the 2s, cast up to original places and turn single (cloverleaf).

B2 2s cast up to first place (improper) while 1s lead down to second place. Then 2s cross over and dance down between the 1s, cast up to first place and turn single (cloverleaf).

The words of the song appear in the Elizabethan play *Wit without Money* by Beaumont & Fletch (Act V, scene iv). The tune, which was later also known as "The Bishop of Chester's Jig" (!), was apparently not published until 1686. It is in the unusual 9/8 or "slip-jig" tempo.

"The fit's upon me now, the fit's upon me now;
Come quickly, gentle lady, the fit's upon me now.
The world shall know they're fools and so shalt thou do too;
Let cobblers mend their tools, the fit's upon me now."

Playford VII
Sharp IV 85
Chappell 176

Duple-minor progressive longways dance for as many as will

Introduction

Men move up a double, turn single and face down; then the Women do likewise, then the Men move down a double, turn single and face the Women's line; then the Women do the same and face the Men.

First Verse

1 and 2 Men fall back a double and come forward again turning single. Then the Women do the same. Partners change places by right shoulders. 1s and 2s change places along the lines by right shoulders. Partners change places by right shoulders.

    Repeat this verse as many times as required to bring the top couple to the foot of the set.

Second Verse

1 and 2 Men change places by doing a two-hand turn once-and-a-half times around, while the Women do the same. 1s face up and 2s face down. All slip sideways four small slips towards partners and turn single in a cloverleaf, separating back to lines as they do. Circle clockwise (hands-four) half-way around and turn single. Do a right-hand star half-way around and turn single.

    Repeat this verse as many times as required to bring the new top couple to the foot of the set.

The ballad of the Friar and the Nun was known in 1592, even if the original words are lost now. Among many sets of words later married to the tune is "All in a misty morning" from *The Beggars' Opera*, a song recently popularized by the English group Steel-eye Span.

"All in a misty morning when cloudy was the weather,
I met with an old man a-clothed all in leather,
A-clothed all in leather and a cap beneath his chin,
Saying 'How d'ye do, and how d'ye do and how d'ye do again.' "

Playford I
Sharp III 95
Chappell 145

Duple-minor longways progressive set for as many as will.

Introduction (optional)
Partners take near hands and lead up a double and fall back again (twice).

The Dance

A1   1s take near hands, lead down through the 2s, separate and cast back to places. Then 1 and 2 Men take near hands and lead across between the 1 and 2 Women, separate and cast back to places.

A2   2s take near hands, lead up through the 1s, separate and cast back to places. Then the 1 and 2 Women take near hands, lead across between the 1 and 2 Men, separate and cast back to places.

B1   1 Man set forward to the 2 Woman and fall back to place turning single; then 1 Woman set forward to the 2 Man and fall back to place turning single.

B2   Take hands-four and circle clockwise half-way around, diminishing the size of the ring at the end so neighbors can fall back improper holding near hands. Then all set moving forwards and change places with partners crossing by right shoulders.

When Playford published this dance in 1698, he divorced it from its original tune and supplied a new Scottish tune instead. Cecil Sharp apparently did not like the new tune, and so he married the dance to the lovely tune "Hunt the Squirrel" from the early eighteenth century. The original tune (Scottish, before 1530) has been restored to the dance here. To this tune, the young King James V of Scotland wrote a song in 1530 about his experiences going around his kingdom in disguise as a beggar to see what his subjects were really thinking. He was known variously as the Geud Man of Ballangigh or the Gaberlunzie Man.

"The pawkie auld carle came over the lea
With many 'Good days' and 'Evens' to me,
Saying 'Good wife, for your courtesie,
Will you lodge a poor silly man?'
The night was cold, the carle was wet,
And down beside the ingle he sat.
My daughter's shoulders he began to pat,
And cadgily ranted and sang."

Playford X
Sharp VI 127

JOG ON   (Moderate-Difficult)   **8 Bars**

Duple-minor progressive longways set for as many as will.

Introduction
Partners take near hands, lead up a double and fall back a double again; set and turn single. Repeat.

First Verse
1 Man, facing down, take partner with two hands, move up a single and down a single plus a little more until the 1 Woman stands between the 2s. 1 Man and the 2s take hands and circle once around with the 1 Woman in the middle. End the circle with the 2s moving up to progressed places above the 1s. Repeat this verse until the original top couple has reached the foot.

Second Verse (two phrases of music)
A1   1s take both hands; 1 Man push 1 Woman down behind 2 Woman and across into 2 Man's place, the 2s moving up. 1s do a two-hand turn once around, ending improper.

A2   1s take two hands; 1 Man push 1 Woman down behind next 2 Man into 2 Woman's place, the 2s moving up. 1s do a two-hand turn once around; ending proper. Repeat this whole verse until the top couple has reached the foot.

Third Verse
1s cross over by right shoulders and stand behind the 2s. The 2s advance a little towards eachother, honour eachother and then move up to progressed places; 1s move forward into 2s' places (improper) and arm right halfway around. Repeat this verse until the top couple has reached the foot.

Fourth Verse
1s cast off while the 2s take near hands and dance up a double and fall back a short double into 1s' places. The 1s, now in the 2s' places, arm left once around. Repeat this verse until the top couple has reached the foot.

Chappell says that the tune is Elizabethan, and its words can be found in Shakespeare's *A Winter's Tale*. The tune is somewhat related to that of "Half Hannikin," and indeed was itself sometimes also known as "Hanskin."

"Jog on, jog on the footpath way
And merrily mount the stile-a.
Your merry heart goes all the day;
Sad hearts tire in a mile-a."

Playford I
Sharp IV
Chappell 211

LADY, LIE NEAR ME (Difficult) 16 Bars

Duple-minor progressive longways set for as many as will.

First Verse

A   Partners take near hands and lead up a double and fall back again.
B   Repeat A.
C & D   Partners set and turn single, twice.

Second Verse (progressive)

A   1 and 2 Men take near hands, fall back (out) a double and come in a double back to places.
B   Women do likewise.
C   1s cast off to second place while 2s move up.
D   1s do a two-hand turn once around.
This verse is repeated until the top couple reaches the foot.

Third Verse

A   Partners side to right shoulders.
B   Partners side to left shoulders.
C & D   Partners set and turn single, twice.

Fourth Verse (progressive)

A   First corners take right hands and change places by doing a turn one-and-a-half times around.
B   Second corners do likewise.
C   1s lead up the middle and cast off around the 2s back to second place (improper).
D   1s do a two-hand turn one-and-a-half times around to change places.
This verse is repeated until the top couple reaches the foot.

Fifth Verse

A   Partners arm right.
B   Partners arm left.
C & D   Partners set and turn single, twice.

Sixth Verse (progressive)

A   1s move forward a double towards eachother, turn about to stand back to back and move forward a double away from eachother, and turn about to face again.
B   Repeat A.
C   1s meet, take two hands and slip four slips down and fall back into second place, the 2s having moved up.
D   Four changes of a circular hey, starting with partners facing.
This verse is repeated until the top couple reaches the foot.

Chappell says that the tune is Elizabethan and is closely related to the song "Phillida Flouts Me." The original words are given here.

"All in the month of May when all things blossom
As in my bed I lay sleep it grew loathsome.
Up I rose and did walk over yon mountains,
Through meadows and through dales, over rocks and fountains.
I heard a voice to sing: 'Sweetheart, come cheer me;
Thou has been long away; lady, lie near me.' "

Playford I
Chappell 182, 184

MAD ROBIN   (Easy-Moderate)   32 Bars

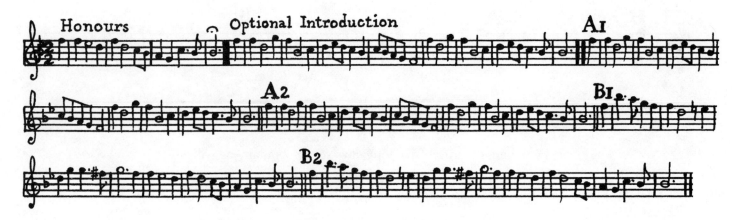

Duple-minor progressive longways set for as many as will.

Introduction (optional)

Partners take near hands and lead up a double and fall back again; repeat.

The Dance

A1   1 Man turns 2 Woman by the right hand, then turns his partner by the left and casts into second place, the 2 Man moving up.

A2   Still in motion at the end of his cast-off, the 1 Man once again turns the 1 Woman by the left, and then she turns the 2 man by the right and casts into second place, the 2 Woman moving up.

B1   Still in motion at the end of her cast-off, the 1 Woman dances up the middle and casts back down again to second place, while the 1 Man shadows her and makes a similar clockwise circle around the 2 Man and back to second place.

B2   Reversing direction, the 1 Man makes a counter-clockwise circle around the 2 Man while the 1 Woman does the same around the 2 Woman.

    Note: in order to make the dance more interesting for the 2s, many dancers have altered B2 so that the 2s make clockwise loops around the 1s—a pleasant change.

Although Chappell could find no copy of "Mad Robin" before the reign of Charles II and Playford did not publish it until 1686, musicologist Christopher Ball claims that at least the tune is Elizabethan. The tune can be found in a collection of English dances (tunes only surviving) assembled by the otherwise unknown Italian dancing-master Gregorio Lambranzi about 1640. Melusine Wood has found longways dances of this degree of complexity from sixteenth-century Italy, so such a dance would not be out of place in Elizabethan England.

Playford VII
Sharp VI 93
Chappell 512

THE NEW FIGARY (Moderate) 32 Bars

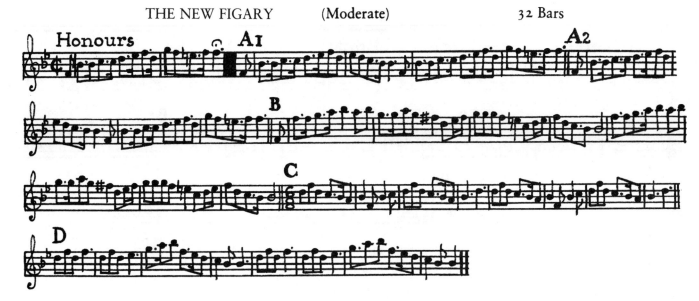

Progressive longways duple-minor set for as many as will.

A1 Partners take near hands and lead up a double and fall back again.

A2 Repeat A1.

B First corners honour and then turn clockwise once around with 2 hands. Second corners honour and then turn clockwise once around.

C First corners back to back, then second corners back to back.

D 1s face down while 2s face up, clap hands on first beat, then clap right hand to right hand on the second, clap hands on the next then clap left hand to left hand on the next; then all turn single (cloverleaf).
All face partners and clap hands on the first beat, then clap right hand to right hand on the second, then clap hands on the next and clap left hand to left hand on the next; 1s cast off into second places while 2s move up.

Playford IV
Sharp III 101

93

NO BODY'S JIG   (Moderate)   32 Bars

Longways Duple-minor for as many as will.

Introduction (optional)

Partners take near hands and lead up a double and fall back to places; then do all that again.

Verses

A1 1s and 2s take hands along the lines by twos, fall back a double and come forward again and meet; then the 1s and 2s make an outward facing ring and go half way around.

A2 Repeat A1 back to places.

B1 1s cross over and cast below the 2s, the 2s moving up. The 1s cross over and cast up to meet above the 2s, the 2s moving down again. Then the 1s lead down to second places while the 2s cast up to first places.

B2 The 2s cross over and cast below the 1s, the 1s moving up. The 2s cross over and cast up to meet above the 1s, the 1s leading down again. The 1s face up and 2s face down, and all set once.

The verses are repeated as many times as desired, but the introduction is only done once.

The tune appears no fewer than three times in the *Fitzwilliam Virginal Book* (first few years of the seventeenth century), which suggests that it had already been well known for several years.

Playford X
Country Dance Book
New Series 11

NO-BODY

SOME-BODY

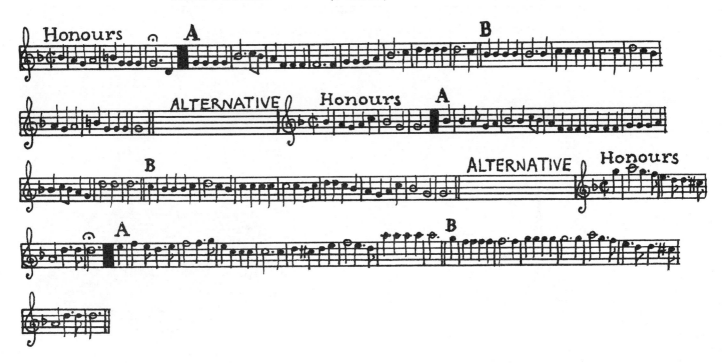

Duple-minor progressive longways set for as many as will.

First Verse

Partners take near hands, lead up a double and fall back again; partners set and turn single. Repeat.

Second Verse (progressive)

1s face down, take near hands and lead forward a double to the 2 Woman; 1 Man takes 2 Woman's left hand in his right hand and then the three of them slip up to first place. The 2 Woman casts off around the 1 Woman, makes a loop through her own place and comes up to first place, and 1 Woman having followed her in the cast and ended up in second place, while the 1 Man casts off to second place, the 2 Man moving up. This verse should be repeated until the top couple has reached the foot.

Third Verse

Partners side to right shoulder, set and turn single; partners side to left shoulder, set and turn single.

Fourth Verse (progressive)

1s face down, take near hands and lead forward to 2 Woman; 1 Man takes 2 Woman's left hand in his right hand and all three slip up to first place. 1 Man kiss 2 Woman's hand, then kiss partner's hand. 1s cast off, 2s moving into first place. Repeat this verse until top couple reaches the foot.

Fifth Verse

Partners arm right, set and turn single. Partners arm left, set and turn single.

Sixth Verse (progressive)

1s face down, take near hands and lead to the 2 Woman; 1 Man takes 2 Woman's left hand in his right hand and all three slip up to first place. 1 Man honours (original says "kiss") 2 Woman, then honours partner. 1s cast off, 2s moving up into first place. Repeat this verse until top couple has reached the foot.

The steeple of the old, gothic St. Paul's Cathedral in London, one of the tallest in the world, was destroyed by fire after being struck by lightning in 1561, and several songs were written to commemorate the event; one, published "at the Sygne of the Hedghogge," appeared only a few days after the fire. Words from one of these songs are given below. Three tunes are offered here, all of them apparently related to eachother in some way. The first tune is taken from Playford I, while the second had an alternative name, "I Am the Duke of Norfolk." The third tune seems to be a variant of the first.

"Lament each one the blazing fire that down from Heaven came,
And burned Saint Paul's his lofty spire with lightning's furious flame.
Lament, I say, both night and day, 'twas London's sins did cause the same.

Playford I
Chappell 117

PAUL'S WHARF   (Moderate)   16 Bars

Duple-minor progressive longways set for as many as will.

First Verse

A1 & 2   Partners lead up a double and fall back again; repeat.

Chorus

B1 & 2   Partners set and turn single; set and turn single again.

Second Verse (progressive)

A1
1s and 2s take hands and circle once around clockwise.
A2
1s take two hands and turn once around as they go down the middle into second place, the 2s moving up.
B1 & 2   Chorus.
        Repeat this verse until top couple reaches the foot.

Third Verse

A1 & 2   Partners side to right shoulders; partners side to left shoulders.
B1 & 2   Chorus.

Fourth Verse (progressive)

A1 & 2   1 and 2 Men take near hands as do 1 and 2 Women; fall back a double then come forward and cross over by right shoulders into partners' places. 1s and 2s take hands and circle half way around counterclockwise into progressed places (note: there is too much music for this, so either move the circle slowly or add a cloverleaf turn single at the end of it).
B1 & 2   Chorus.
            Repeat this verse until top couple reaches the foot.

Fifth Verse

A1 & 2   Partners arm right; partners arm left.
B1 & 2   Chorus.

Sixth Verse (progressive)

A1 & 2   1 and 2 Men do a two-hand skipping turn once-and-a-half around while the 1 and 2 Women do the same. Then all turn single, Men to left and Women to right; then all turn single, reversing direction.
B1 & 2   Chorus.
            Repeat this verse until top couple reaches foot.

Paul's Wharf was one of the public landing-places for picking up fresh water along the Thames River, near St. Paul's Cathedral. Chappell says the tune is Elizabethan.

Playford I
Chappell 130

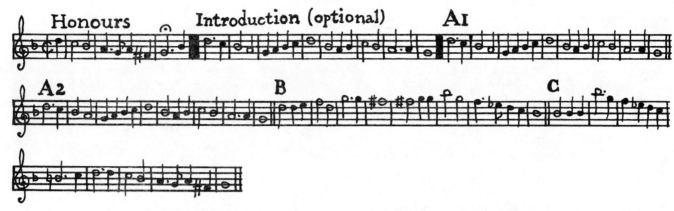

Duple-minor progressive longways set for as many as will.

Introduction (optional)

Partners take near hands and lead up a double and fall back again; Repeat.

The Dance

A1   First corners side to right shoulders, set and turn single.

A2   Second corners side to left shoulders, set and turn single.

B   First corners change places by right shoulders; then second corners change. All fall back a single and come forward, crossing by right shoulders and changing places with partners. All are now progressed and proper.

C   Right-hand star once around, then all turn single.

Chappell suggests a connection between "The Queen's Jig" and an Elizabethan tune (Trinity College, Dublin MS412, fol.23r). The dance itself was not published until 1701, at which time it was accompanied by a fine eighteenth-century tune beloved of many dancers. The Elizabethan tune is given here. The question then presents itself: who is the Queen of "The Queen's Jig?" In 1701, the stolid Mary II had been dead over five years, and Anne would not be crowned for another year when her brother-in-law William III died; thus, naming the dance after Mary or Anne would have been tasteless and pointless. The revival, however, in 1701 of an Elizabethan dance named after Queen Elizabeth, who loved to dance, would have been quite proper.

"Care go thou away from me for I am not fit mated for thee.
Thou borest me of my wits, wherefore I behold thy frantic fits.
Therefore I could care no more since my care cannot restore,
But I shall sing a-down, a-down, a-dee
And cast away care, far away from me."

Playford XI
Sharp VI 106
Chappell 689

ROW WELL, YE MARINERS   (Moderate)   24 Bars

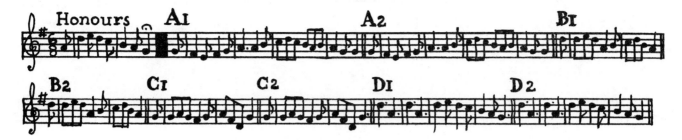

Duple-minor progressive longways set for as many as will.

First Verse
A1   Partners take near hands and lead up a double and fall back again.
A2   Repeat A1.

Chorus
B1   1s facing up, 1 Man slips two slips to his left, then Woman slips two slips to her right.
B2   1 Man slips back to place, then 1 Woman slips back to place.
C1   1s and 2s take near hands along the lines; all fall back a double.
C2   All come forward a double to places.
D1   Partners do a series of hand-claps: their own; partner right to right; their own; partner left to left; their own; their own breast; both partner's hands.
D2   Repeat D1, but doing left-to-left before right-to-right.

Second Verse (progressive)
A1   1s and 2s side to right shoulders along the lines.
A2   1s and 2s honour and then change places along the lines, Men passing by left shoulders and Women passing by right shoulders.
B-D   Chorus.
     This verse is repeated as many times as desired.

Playford's description of the Second Verse is badly garbled, so Sharp's interpretation is followed here. The song was first published in 1565, and the tune was used many times to set various words, some moralizing, some political and some scurrilous. Most of the earliest sets of words have been lost, so none is reproduced here, except to say that the words of each D section were "Row well, row well, row well, ye mariners."

Playford I
Sharp III 102
Chappell 112

Duple-minor progressive longways set for as many as will.

First Verse

A1   Partners take near hands, lead up a double and fall back again; partners set and turn single.

A2   Repeat A1

B1   1s meet and fall back, then do a skipping two-hand turn one-and-a-half times around; 1s face down and 2s face up; all set.

B2   1s meet and fall back, then do a skipping two-hand turn one-and-a-half times around back to places; 1s change places with 2s, passing by right shoulders. Repeat this verse until the original top couple reaches the foot.

Second Verse

A1   Partners side to right shoulders, set and turn single.

A2   Partners side to left shoulders, set and turn single.

B1   1s and 2s take near hands along the lines and fall back a double; then cross over by right shoulders and change places with partners.

B2   1 Man and 2 Woman go into the middle and stand back to back; then 2 Man and 1 Woman do likewise; take hands in an outward-facing circle and move clockwise half-way around and fall into progressed places. Repeat this verse until top couple reaches the foot.

Third Verse

A1   Partners arm right, set and turn single.

A2   Partners arm left, set and turn single.

B1   1s come forward a double, meet and fall back a double, then cast into second place, the 2s moving up.

B2   1s do a full figure-8 up through the 2s.
      Repeat this verse until top couple reaches the foot.

Two tunes are given for this dance; they are actually almost identical, except that the first one is in a minor key and the second in a major key. Sharp borrowed the former to accompany "Jacob Hall's Jig" (from Playford IX, 1695), so it is already well known to many dancers. The minor tune is associated with the song "Under and Over" and the major tune with "Jones' Ale" which, published in 1594, was also known as "The Jovial Tinker." The latter title is given by Ben Jonson in *Tale of a Tub* (1633) as the name of a dance, while "Under and Over" is a dance published by Playford in 1652; it is most probable that the two dances were one and the same. "Jones' Ale" was also sung to a completely different tune at least as early as 1628, to which is appended a chorus, and it is this version of this jolly, humorous song that continues as one of the favorites of the British traditional folk-music revival.

"As abroad I was walking I heard two lovers talking,
One to another speaking of lovers' constancy.
As in a meadow turning upon a summer's morning
I heard these lovers mourning cause of love's cruelty.
For under and over, over and under, under and over again
Quoth she, "Sweetheart, I love thee as maidens should love men."

"There was a jovial tinker who was no small-beer drinker;
He never was a shrinker to make up a jovial crew.
And he came all the way from the Weald of Kent,
And when all his money was gone and spent
It made him look like Jack-a-lent,
When Jones' Ale was new, when Jones' ale was new, my boys,
When Jones' Ale was new."
      chorus of the completely different tune:
"And they called for their pints of beer and bottles of sherry
To help them over the hills so merry,
To help them over the hills so merry,
When Jones' Ale was new, my boys, when Jones' ale was new."

Playford II
Chappell 187, 189

BASILINA   (Moderate)   28 Bars

[no tune known]

Processional Double Circle, Women on inside, all facing clockwise.

4 bars A	Partners take near hands and dance forward a double and back a double.
3 bars B1	Partners dance forward a double and back a single.
B2	Partners dance five steps forward and close.
B3	Partners face, set to the right, set to the left, and, facing clockwise, set (a single) to the right.
A2	Partners lead forward a double and fall back a double.
B4	Partners lead forward a double and fall back a single.
A3 & 4	Partners lead forward four doubles.

No music has yet been identified as belonging to this dance. The dance directions, somewhat ambiguous in wording, survive in a manuscript from the Inns of Court, MS Douce 280 at the Bodleian Library, Oxford. The dance is known to have been danced in Henry VIII's time, and was still going strong in 1596, when mentioned by Nashe, and in about 1606 when the Douce manuscript was compiled.

Chappell 116
Cunningham 28

THE BLACK ALMAIN   (Moderate-Difficult)

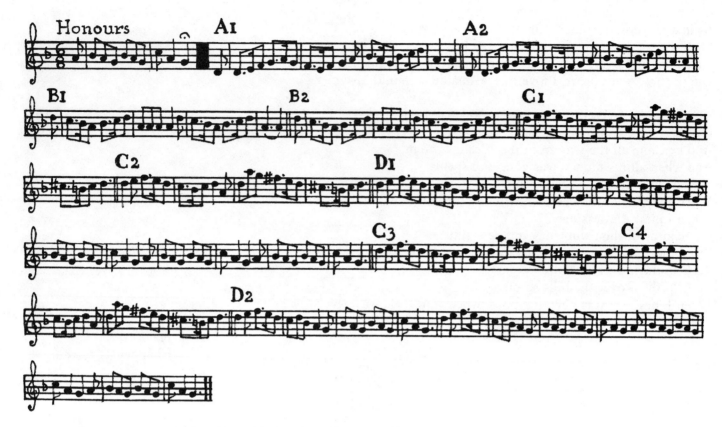

Processional Double Circle, Women on the inside, all facing clockwise.

A1 & 2 Partners take near hands and dance four doubles clockwise around the circle, ending with partners facing; drop hands.

B1 All fall back a double away from partner, then come forward to places.

B2 All face left and dance a double around the circle (Men clockwise and Women counter-clockwise); reverse directions and dance a double back to meet partners; face partners.

C1 Men set and turn single.

C2 Women set and turn single.

D1 Partners take both hands and do a counter-clockwise turn three-quarters around in a double step. Partners place hands on eachother's shoulders and slip four slips to the outside; then do a two-hand turn half-way around clockwise in a double step; partners place hands on eachother's shoulders and slip four slips back to places, ending with Men in outer ring facing partners in inner ring. Drop hands and fall back a double away from partners and then come forward a double again.

C3 Repeat C1

C4 Repeat C2

D2 Repeat D1

This dance appears in many early manuscripts: British Library, Harley 367 (16th century); Bodleian Library Oxford, Douce 280 (ca. 1606); Inner Temple Library Miscellanea Vol. XXVII (mid-seventeenth century); Royal College of Music, MS.1119 (mid-seventeenth century). A 1570 broadside calls for the "newe tune of the Blacke Almaine" The following sixteenth-century words were to be sung to this tune:

" 'Maid, will you marry?' 'I pray, sir, tarry; I am not disposed to wed-a;
For he that shall have me, will never deny me, he shall have my maidenhead-a.'
'Why then, you will not wed me?' 'No, sure, sire, I have sped me.'
'You must go seek some other wight that better may your heart delight;
Believe me it grieves me I may not have you, to wed and bed you as a woman should be.' "

Pugliese 31
Cunningham, appendix

Processional Double Circle, women on inside, all facing clockwise.

A1   Partners take near hands and lead up a double, followed by a single setting step backwards to the right. Lead up a further double, followed by a single setting step backwards to the left.

A2   Repeat A1

B   Partners drop hands and face eachother and set to eachother, then take near hands and lead clockwise a double, followed by a slow set (backwards to the right) and honour.

The dance is repeated as many times as desired.

The description of the dance given here is based on the manuscript Douce 280 at the Bodleian Library, Oxford. The B section is slightly different in all the other surviving manuscript descriptions, but this is the version that fits the music best. The other references are: Rawl. Poet. 108 (ca. 1570) and Rawl. D. 864 (ca. 1630), both at the Bodleian; Harley 367 (undated but thought to be about 1570) at the British Library; the Inner Temple Miscellanea XXVII, and the Royal College of Music Ms. 1119, where the tune was found.

    The Measure is an ancient English dance form, going back to the days of village waits (thus prompting a pun), and some were danced in 8-bar phrases rather than 6-bar phrases as here. Mabel Dolmetsch found an untitled Measure tune in the Giles Lodge Lute Book manuscript (1570) at the Folger Shakespeare Library in Washington, DC, with 8-bar phrases.

    The Earl of Essex was Robert Devereux (1567-1601), a favorite of Queen Elizabeth; he had to be executed for high treason.

Mabel Dolmetsch 49ff
Pugliese 17-18.
Cunningham appendix

Processional Double Circle, Women on the inside, all facing clockwise.

A1   Partners take near hands, lead forward a double and fall back a double to places; partners face, take right hands and do an "Althea" balance* starting on the right foot; drop hands and turn single; take left hands and do an "Althea" balance, starting on the left foot; drop hands and turn single.

A2   All face clockwise, take near hands and lead forward a double and fall back a double; all face counter-clockwise, take near hands, lead forward a double and fall back a double. All face clockwise again, lead forward a double and fall back a double.

B   Partners face, take right hands and do an "Althea" balance, starting on the right foot; drop hands and turn single. Partners take left hands and do an "Althea" balance, starting on the left foot; drop hands and turn single.

* The "Althea" balance, as found in the Elizabethan country dance "Althea," is similar to the more recent New England contra balance: step onto the right foot and kick to the right with the left foot, then step onto the left foot and kick to the left with the right foot.

This dance appears in many early manuscripts: British Library, Harley 367 (sixteenth century); Bodleian Library, Oxford, Rawl. Poet. 108 (ca. 1570), Douce 280 (ca. 1606), Rawl. D. 864 (ca. 1630); Inner Temple Library Miscellanea Vol. XXVII (mid-seventeenth century); Royal College of Music, MS 1119 (mid-seventeenth century).

Pugliese 19
Cunningham appendix

TURKELONEY   (Moderate)   **24 Bars**

Double Circle, Women on inside, all facing clockwise.

A1   Partners take near hands and lead forward a double with long steps and fall, back a double with small steps, then go forward a double again and fall back again.

A2   Repeat A1.

B1   Partners drop hands and face and set to eachother. Then face clockwise and take near hands and lead forward a double.

B2   Fall back a double with small steps, then drop hands and face and set to eachother.

The dance is repeated as many times as desired.

The figure of this dance is described in many early manuscripts, including Rawl. Poet. 108 (ca. 1570), Douce 280 (ca. 1606), Rawl. D. 864 (ca. 1630), all at the Bodleian Library, Oxford; the Inner Temple Library Miscellania XXVII, and the Royal College of Music Ms. 1119, both dated mid-seventeenth century; Harley 367 at the British Library, undated but believed to be from about 1570. The music can be found in William Ballet's Lute Book (Library of Trinity College, Dublin, late 16th century). The earliest surviving reference to the dance can be dated to 1557-8, and an early seventeenth-century manuscript in a private collection available to Chappell associates the tune with an entertaining set of words that were first published in 1557:

"If ever I marry, I'll marry a maid;
To marry a widow I'm sore afraid.
For maids they are simple and never will grudge
But widows full oft, as they say, know too much."

Chappell 95
Melusine Wood
Pugliese 14-15
Cunningham appendix

THE FARANDOLE (Easy)

The set for a Farandole is a single file of dancers each holding hands, and the more dancers the merrier. The leader takes them with either a walking or a running step wherever he or she wills, usually tracing geometric figures on the ground. The leader may have one couple make an arch and then lead the file through the arch (called "threading the needle"). The leader may lead the file into a tight spiral and then it out through a series of arches. The dance can be accompanied by almost any music.

The Farandole, which is known to have been danced in Italy and Provence (now southern France) in the twelfth century and is still being widely danced today by children and their elders, was danced in sixteenth-century England. It is still considered to be the national or regional dance of Provence today. Rubens painted a picture of country dancers doing the farandole early in the seventeenth century, an engraving of which may be found in the collection of the College of William & Mary.

In Stanza LXIII of Sir John Davies' poem "Orchestra", written while he was a student at the Inns of Court in 1595, is this description of a Farandole in Elizabethan England:

"As when a nymph arysing from the land
Leadeth a daunce with her long watery traine
Downe to the Sea, she wries to every hand,
And every way doth crosse the fertile plaine:
But when at last she falls into the Maine,
Then all her traverses concluded are,
And with the Sea her course is circulare."

Melusine Wood 5ff, 101

106

ALL FLOWERS OF THE BROOM

16 Bars

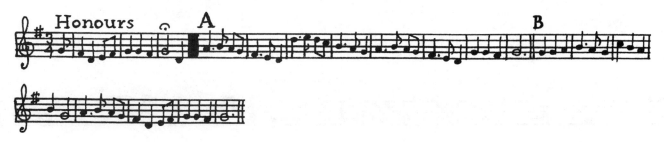

This dance, which is not to be confused with "Broom, the Broom, the Bonny, Bonny Broom," is known to have been danced as early as 1577. The tune is found in William Ballet's Lute Book.

Chappell 116

BARLEY BREAK

32 Bars

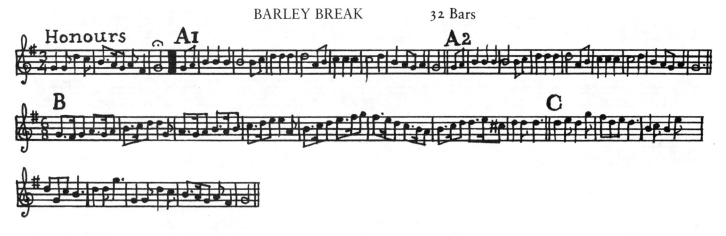

"Barley Break" was an outdoor game quite popular among young Elizabethans. It was also the name of a country dance, for which the tune can be found in *My Lady Neville's Virginal Book*, dated 1591. The tune is unusual for this period in having a section in three-four tempo, like the "Cushion Dance."

Chappell 135

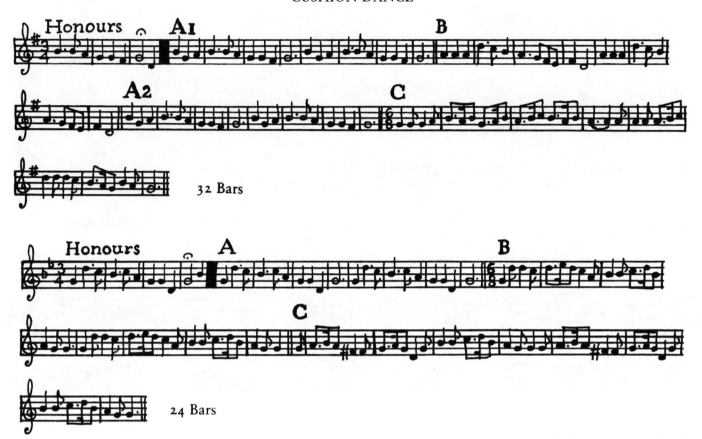

32 Bars

24 Bars

Chappel gives two different tunes for the "Cushion Dance," which, like "Barley Break," have a characteristic pattern of three-four time followed by six-eight time. The first tune was published in Amsterdam in 1615 and the other was included in the 1686 edition of Playford, but the dance seems to have been almost exclusively a sixteenth-century form, so it may safely be assumed that the tunes were already old when published.

Chappell quotes from the 1686 Playford description of the theory behind this dance, but the actual figures danced by the circle of dancers must remain a mystery, since Playford did not describe them. The dance begins when someone (man or woman) picks out a partner and lays a cushion at that person's feet.

"This dance is begun by a single person (either man or woman), who, taking a cushion in hand, dances about the room, and at the end of the tune, stops and sings, 'This dance it will no further go." The musician answers, 'I pray you, good Sir, why say you so?'—*Man.* 'Because Joan Sanderson will not come too.'—*Musician.* 'She must come too, and she shall come too, and she must come whether she will or no.' Then he lays down the cushion before the woman, on which she kneels, and he kisses her, singing 'Welcome, Joan Sanderson, welcome, welcome.' Then she rises, takes up the cushion, and both dance, singing, 'Prinkum-prankum is a fine dance, and shall we go dance it once again, once again, and once again, and shall we go dance it once again.' Then making a stop, the *woman* sings as before, 'This dance it will no further go.'—*Musician.* 'I pray you, madam, why say you so?'—*Woman.* 'Because *John* Sanderson will not come too.'—*Musician.* 'He must come too, and he shall come too, and he must come whether he will or no.' And so she lays down the cushion before a man, who kneeling upon it, salutes her; she singing, 'Welcome, John Sanderson, welcome, welcome.' Then he taking up the cushion, they take hands, and dance round, singing as before. And thus they do, till the whole company are taken into the ring; and if there is company enough, make a little ring in its middle, and within that ring, set a chair, and lay the cushion in it, and the first man set in it. Then the cushion is laid before the first man, the woman singing, 'This dance it will no further go;' and as before, only instead of 'Come too,' they sing, 'Go fro;' and instead of 'Welcome, John Sanderson,' they sing, 'Farewell, John Sanderson, farewell, farewell;' and so they go out one by one as they came in. NOTE.—*The women are kissed by all the men in the ring at their coming and going out, and likewise the men by all the women.*"

The Dancing Master of 1686

Chappell 153ff

William Webbe in his *Discourse of English Poetrie* (1586) mentions three country dances by name, including one called Downright Squire. No dance or tune of that name has so far been discovered, but a song called The Upright Esquier appears in a manuscript of the period at the Folger Shakespeare Library (ms. 448.16 ff. 18v - 19), and it surely must be the tune to which Webbe refers. The tune in the manuscript is slightly garbled and has required a small amount of reconstruction here.

"You lordings, cast off your weedes of wo; me thinks I heare
A trumpet shril which plain doth show my Lord is neare;
Tantaratara tantara.
This trumpet glads our hearts;
Therefore to welcome home your king, you lordings plaie your parts;
Tantaratara tantara.
You lordings plaie your parts."

I CARE NOT FOR THESE LADIES   20 Bars

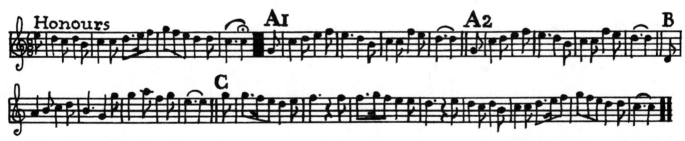

This jolly dance-tune was published in Thomas Campion's *A Book of Ayres* (1601), although Campion probably did not write the tune. No original dance instructions or even references have been found. However, various twentieth-century country-dances have been written for the tune, and one of them in the Elizabethan style (by Kitty Creelman Skrobela, and published in *Country Dance & Song*, 1969 #2) has been adapted here, as the movements of the dance so nicely reflect the title.

Circular set for as many as will. Three verses: 1) Take hands and go into the middle a double and back, twice. 2) Side to right and then to left shoulders. 3) Arm right and arm left. CHORUS: B, partners set and turn single; C, 4 changes of a Grand Chain (2 beats each) and turn the fifth person once around with two hands.

"I care not for these ladies that must be wooed and prayed;
Give me kind Amarillis, the wanton country maid;
Nature art disdaineth; her beauty is her own.
For when we court and kiss she cries "Forsooth, let go,"
But when we come where comfort is she never will say no.

JOHN COME KISS ME NOW 16 Bars

Mentioned as a popular dance in Heywood's *A Woman Kill'd with Kindness*, 1600, this dance was occasionally also called "Joan, Come Kiss Me Now."

"John, come kiss me now, now, now;
John, come kiss me now, now, now;
John, come kiss me by and by,
And make no more ado."

Chappell 147

MALL SIMS 20 Bars

The earliest publication of the tune is in Morley's *Consort Lessons*, 1599, but the dance (and presumably the tune) existed long before that. Chappell observes that the tune is characteristic of traditional music for the harp.

Chappell 177, 789

The earliest surviving publication of this tune is in *A New Book of Tablature*, 1596, but it may be considerably older than that. It is said to be named after Sir John Packington (1549-1625), an eccentric who wagered that he could swim from Westminster to Greenwich (several miles down the Thames River), but Queen Elizabeth would not permit the long-distance swim. He constructed a "pownde" (pond), and when he was confronted with complaints that the pond was built across a public highway he breached the embankment and flooded the surrounding area. The tune was used over the next two centuries for many satirical songs. The dance is believed to have been in the form of a circle for as many as will, similar to Sellenger's Round.

Chappell 123

A STEWPOND. Containing perch, carp, tench or lampreys, they were used in great houses and monastic foundations as a source of fresh fish.

PEGGY RAMSEY 16 Bars

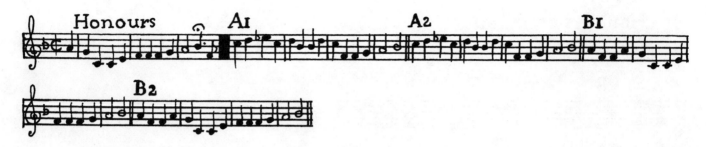

The dance is mentioned in Shakespeare's *Twelfth Night* (Act II, scene iii) and elsewhere in sixteenth-century literature. The tune is given in William Ballet's Lute Book, although Chappell shows that the song had an alternate tune. It is sometimes called "Peg a Ramsey" or "Peg of Ramsey," Ramsey being a little town in Huntingdonshire.

"When I was a bachelor, I led a merry life;
But now I am a married man and troubled with a wife.
I cannot do as I have done because I live in fear:
If I but go to Islington my wife is watching there."

Chappell 218

RURAL DANCE ABOUT THE MAYPOLE 16 Bars

The earliest record of this dance is that it was danced at Mr. Young's ball in May 1671, but it is likely to be a century or more older than that. The words given by Chappell, however, are likely to be from the seventeenth century:

"You lasses and lads, take leave of your Dads,
And away to the Maypole hie;
There every he has got him a she,
And the minstrels standing by.
For Willy has got his Jill and Jonnie has his Joan,
To trip it, trip it, trip it, trip it, trip it up and down."

Chappell 531

This dance, whose figures have not survived, was mentioned in a letter prefixed to Anthony Munday's translation of *Gerileon in England*, part ii, 1592, and in Henry Chettle's pamplet, *Kind-hart's Dreame*, also printed in 1592. The tune can be found in the *Fitzwilliam Virginal Book*, compiled early in the seventeenth century. Because the words relate to the song as a dance, two verses are given here, the first and seventh:

"There was a maid this other day
And she would needs go forth to play;
And as she walked she sighed and said,
'I am afraid to die a maid.'
When that be-heard a lad what talk this maiden had
Thereof he was full glad and did not spare
To say, 'Fair maid, I pray, whither go you to play?'
'Good sir,' then did she say, 'what do you care?'
'For I will without fail, Maiden, give you Watkin's Ale.'
'Watkin's Ale, good Sir,' quoth she, 'what is that? I pray, tell me.'

Thrice scarcely changed hath the moon
Since first this pretty trick was done;
Which being heard of one by chance,
He made thereof a Country Dance.
And as I heard the tale, he called it Watkin's Ale,
Which never will be stale, I do believe.
This dance is now in prime and chiefly us'd this time,
And latrly put in rhime; let no man grieve
To hear this merry jesting tale, the which is called Watkin's Ale:
It is not long since it was made; the finest flower will soonest fade."

Chappell, 136-7